U.S. Fish & Wildlife Service

Adaptive Harvest Management

2008 Hunting Season

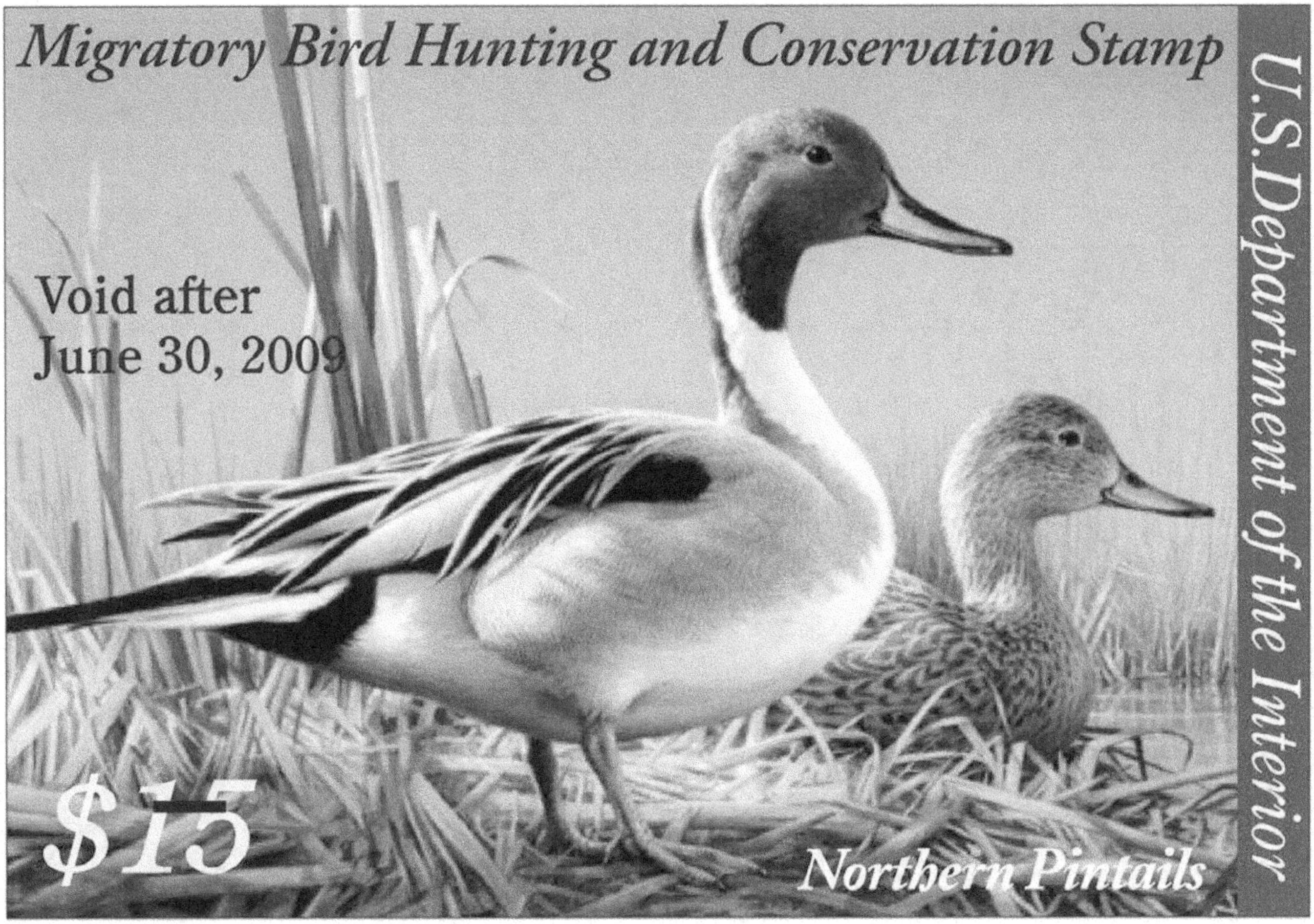
Migratory Bird Hunting and Conservation Stamp
U.S. Department of the Interior
Void after
June 30, 2009
$15
Northern Pintails

Adaptive Harvest Management

2008 Hunting Season

PREFACE

The process of setting waterfowl hunting regulations is conducted annually in the United States (Blohm 1989). This process involves a number of meetings where the status of waterfowl is reviewed by the agencies responsible for setting hunting regulations. In addition, the U.S. Fish and Wildlife Service (USFWS) publishes proposed regulations in the *Federal Register* to allow public comment. This document is part of a series of reports intended to support development of harvest regulations for the 2008 hunting season. Specifically, this report is intended to provide waterfowl managers and the public with information about the use of adaptive harvest management (AHM) for setting waterfowl hunting regulations in the United States. This report provides the most current data, analyses, and decision-making protocols. However, adaptive management is a dynamic process and some information presented in this report will differ from that in previous reports.

Citation: U.S. Fish and Wildlife Service. 2008. Adaptive Harvest Management: 2008 Hunting Season. U.S. Dept. Interior, Washington, D.C. 54pp. Available online at http://www.fws.gov/migratorybirds/mgmt/AHM/AHM-intro htm

ACKNOWLEDGMENTS

A working group comprised of representatives from the USFWS, the U.S. Geological Survey (USGS), the Canadian Wildlife Service (CWS), and the four Flyway Councils (Appendix 1) was established in 1992 to review the scientific basis for managing waterfowl harvests. The working group, supported by technical experts from the waterfowl management and research communities, subsequently proposed a framework for adaptive harvest management, which was first implemented in 1995. The USFWS expresses its gratitude to the AHM Working Group and to the many other individuals, organizations, and agencies that have contributed to the development and implementation of AHM.

This report was prepared by the USFWS Division of Migratory Bird Management. G. S. Boomer and T. A. Sanders were the principal authors. Individuals that provided essential information or otherwise assisted with report preparation were F. Johnson (USGS), M. Runge (USGS), M. Koneff (USFWS), K. Richkus (USFWS), T. Liddick (USFWS), E. Silverman (USFWS), N. Zimpfer (USFWS), J. Klimstra (USFWS), A. Royle (USGS), and P. Garrettson (USFWS). Comments regarding this document should be sent to the Chief, Division of Migratory Bird Management - USFWS, 4401 North Fairfax Drive, MS MSP-4107, Arlington, VA 22203.

TABLE OF CONTENTS

EXECUTIVE SUMMARY

In 1995 the U.S. Fish and Wildlife Service (USFWS) implemented the Adaptive Harvest Management (AHM) program for setting duck hunting regulations in the United States. The AHM approach provides a framework for making objective decisions in the face of incomplete knowledge concerning waterfowl population dynamics and regulatory impacts.

This year the AHM protocol is based on the population dynamics and status of three mallard (*Anas platyrhynchos*) stocks. Mid-continent mallards are defined as those breeding in the Waterfowl Breeding Population and Habitat Survey (WBPHS) strata 13–18, 20–50, and 75–77 plus mallards breeding in the states of Michigan, Minnesota, and Wisconsin (state surveys). The prescribed regulatory alternative for the Mississippi and Central Flyways depends exclusively on the status of these mallards. Eastern mallards are defined as those breeding in WBPHS strata 51–54, and 56 and breeding in the states of Virginia northward into New Hampshire (Atlantic Flyway Breeding Waterfowl Survey [AFBWS]). The regulatory choice for the Atlantic Flyway depends exclusively on the status of these mallards. Western mallards are defined as those birds breeding in WBPHS strata 1–12 (hereafter Alaska) and those birds breeding in the states of California and Oregon (state surveys). The regulatory choice for the Pacific Flyway depends exclusively on the status of these mallards.

Mallard population models are based on the best available information and account for uncertainty in population dynamics and the impact of harvest. Model-specific weights reflect the relative confidence in alternative hypotheses and are updated annually using comparisons of predicted and observed population sizes. For mid-continent mallards, current model weights favor the weakly density-dependent reproductive hypothesis (85%) and suggest some preference for the additive-mortality hypothesis (62%). For eastern mallards, virtually all of the weight is on models that have corrections for bias in estimates of survival or reproductive rates. Model weights do not discriminate between the strongly density-dependent (46%) and weakly density-dependent (54%) reproductive hypotheses. By consensus, hunting mortality is assumed to be additive in eastern mallards. Unlike mid-continent and eastern mallards, we consider a single functional form to predict western mallard population dynamics but consider a wide range of parameter values each weighted relative to the support from the data.

For the 2008 hunting season, the USFWS is considering the same regulatory alternatives as last year. The nature of the restrictive, moderate, and liberal alternatives has remained essentially unchanged since 1997, except that extended framework dates have been offered in the moderate and liberal alternatives since 2002. Harvest rates associated with each of the regulatory alternatives have been updated based on band-reporting rate studies conducted since 1998. Estimated harvest rates of adult males from the 2002–2007 liberal hunting seasons have averaged 0.105 (SE = 0.003), 0.133 (SE = 0.008), 0.109 (SE = 0.004). for mid-continent, eastern and western mallards, respectively. The estimated marginal effect of framework-date extensions has been an increase in harvest rate of 0.006 (SD = 0.008) and 0.004 (SD = 0.010) for mid-continent and eastern mallards, respectively.

Optimal regulatory strategies for the 2008 hunting season were calculated using: (1) harvest-management objectives specific to each mallard stock; (2) the 2008 regulatory alternatives; and (3) current population models. Based on this year's survey results of 7.87 million mid-continent mallards, 3.05 million ponds in Prairie Canada, 815 thousand eastern mallards, and 914 thousand western mallards in Alaska (532 thousand) and California-Oregon (381 thousand), the optimal choice for all four flyways is the liberal regulatory alternative.

AHM concepts and tools are also being applied to help improve harvest management for several other waterfowl stocks. In the last year, progress has been made in understanding the harvest potential of American black ducks (*Anas rubripes*), the Atlantic Population of Canada geese (*Branta canadensis*), northern pintails (*Anas acuta*), and scaup (*Aythya affinis, A. marila*). While these biological assessments are on-going, they are already informing decision makers and proving valuable in helping focus debate on the social aspects of harvesting policy, including management objectives and the nature of regulatory alternatives.

BACKGROUND

The annual process of setting duck-hunting regulations in the United States is based on a system of resource monitoring, data analyses, and rule-making (Blohm 1989). Each year, monitoring activities such as aerial surveys and hunter questionnaires provide information on population size, habitat conditions, and harvest levels. Data collected from this monitoring program are analyzed each year, and proposals for duck-hunting regulations are developed by the Flyway Councils, States, and USFWS. After extensive public review, the USFWS announces regulatory guidelines within which States can set their hunting seasons.

In 1995, the USFWS adopted the concept of adaptive resource management (Walters 1986) for regulating duck harvests in the United States. This approach explicitly recognizes that the consequences of hunting regulations cannot be predicted with certainty and provides a framework for making objective decisions in the face of that uncertainty (Williams and Johnson 1995). Inherent in the adaptive approach is an awareness that management performance can be maximized only if regulatory effects can be predicted reliably. Thus, adaptive management relies on an iterative cycle of monitoring, assessment, and decision-making to clarify the relationships among hunting regulations, harvests, and waterfowl abundance.

In regulating waterfowl harvests, managers face four fundamental sources of uncertainty (Nichols et al. 1995*a*, Johnson et al. 1996, Williams et al. 1996):

(1)   environmental variation - the temporal and spatial variation in weather conditions and other key features of waterfowl habitat; an example is the annual change in the number of ponds in the Prairie Pothole Region, where water conditions influence duck reproductive success;

(2)   partial controllability - the ability of managers to control harvest only within limits; the harvest resulting from a particular set of hunting regulations cannot be predicted with certainty because of variation in weather conditions, timing of migration, hunter effort, and other factors;

(3)   partial observability - the ability to estimate key population attributes (e.g., population size, reproductive rate, harvest) only within the precision afforded by extant monitoring programs; and

(4)   structural uncertainty - an incomplete understanding of biological processes; a familiar example is the long-standing debate about whether harvest is additive to other sources of mortality or whether populations compensate for hunting losses through reduced natural mortality. Structural uncertainty increases contentiousness in the decision-making process and decreases the extent to which managers can meet long-term conservation goals.

AHM was developed as a systematic process for dealing objectively with these uncertainties. The key components of AHM include (Johnson et al. 1993, Williams and Johnson 1995):

(1)   a limited number of regulatory alternatives, which describe Flyway-specific season lengths, bag limits, and framework dates;

(2)   a set of population models describing various hypotheses about the effects of harvest and environmental factors on waterfowl abundance;

(3)   a measure of reliability (probability or "weight") for each population model; and

(4)   a mathematical description of the objective(s) of harvest management (i.e., an "objective function"), by which alternative regulatory strategies can be compared.

These components are used in a stochastic optimization procedure to derive a regulatory strategy. A regulatory strategy specifies the optimal regulatory choice, with respect to the stated management objectives, for each possible combination of breeding population size, environmental conditions, and model weights (Johnson et al. 1997). The setting of annual hunting regulations then involves an iterative process:

(1)   each year, an optimal regulatory choice is identified based on resource and environmental conditions, and on current model weights;

4

(2)   after the regulatory decision is made, model-specific predictions for subsequent breeding population size are determined;

(3)   when monitoring data become available, model weights are increased to the extent that observations of population size agree with predictions, and decreased to the extent that they disagree; and

(4)   the new model weights are used to start another iteration of the process.

By iteratively updating model weights and optimizing regulatory choices, the process should eventually identify which model is the best overall predictor of changes in population abundance. The process is optimal in the sense that it provides the regulatory choice each year necessary to maximize management performance. It is adaptive in the sense that the harvest strategy "evolves" to account for new knowledge generated by a comparison of predicted and observed population sizes.

MALLARD STOCKS AND FLYWAY MANAGEMENT

Since its inception AHM has focused on the population dynamics and harvest potential of mallards, especially those breeding in mid-continent North America. Mallards constitute a large portion of the total U.S. duck harvest, and traditionally have been a reliable indicator of the status of many other species. As management capabilities have grown, there has been increasing interest in the ecology and management of breeding mallards that occur outside the mid-continent region. Geographic differences in the reproduction, mortality, and migrations of mallard stocks suggest that there may be corresponding differences in optimal levels of sport harvest. The ability to regulate harvests of mallards originating from various breeding areas is complicated, however, by the fact that a large degree of mixing occurs during the hunting season. The challenge for managers, then, is to vary hunting regulations among Flyways in a manner that recognizes each Flyway's unique breeding-ground derivation of mallards. Of course, no Flyway receives mallards exclusively from one breeding area, therefore Flyway-specific harvest strategies ideally should account for multiple breeding stocks that are exposed to a common harvest.

The optimization procedures used in AHM can account for breeding populations of mallards beyond the mid-continent region, and for the manner in which these ducks distribute themselves among the Flyways during the hunting season. An optimal approach would allow for Flyway-specific regulatory strategies, which in a sense represent for each Flyway an average of the optimal harvest strategies for each contributing breeding stock, weighted by the relative size of each stock in the fall flight. This joint optimization of multiple mallard stocks requires: (1) models of population dynamics for all recognized stocks of mallards; (2) an objective function that accounts for harvest-management goals for all mallard stocks in the aggregate; and (3) decision rules allowing Flyway-specific regulatory choices.

Currently, three stocks of mallards are officially recognized for the purposes of AHM (Fig. 1). We use a constrained approach to the optimization of these stocks' harvest, in which the Atlantic Flyway regulatory strategy is based exclusively on the status of eastern mallards, the regulatory strategy for the Mississippi and Central Flyways is based exclusively on the status of mid-continent mallards, and the Pacific Flyway regulatory strategy is based exclusively on the status of western mallards. This approach has been determined to perform nearly as well as a joint-optimization because mixing of the three stocks during the hunting season is limited and because of the constraints imposed by management objectives and regulatory alternatives.

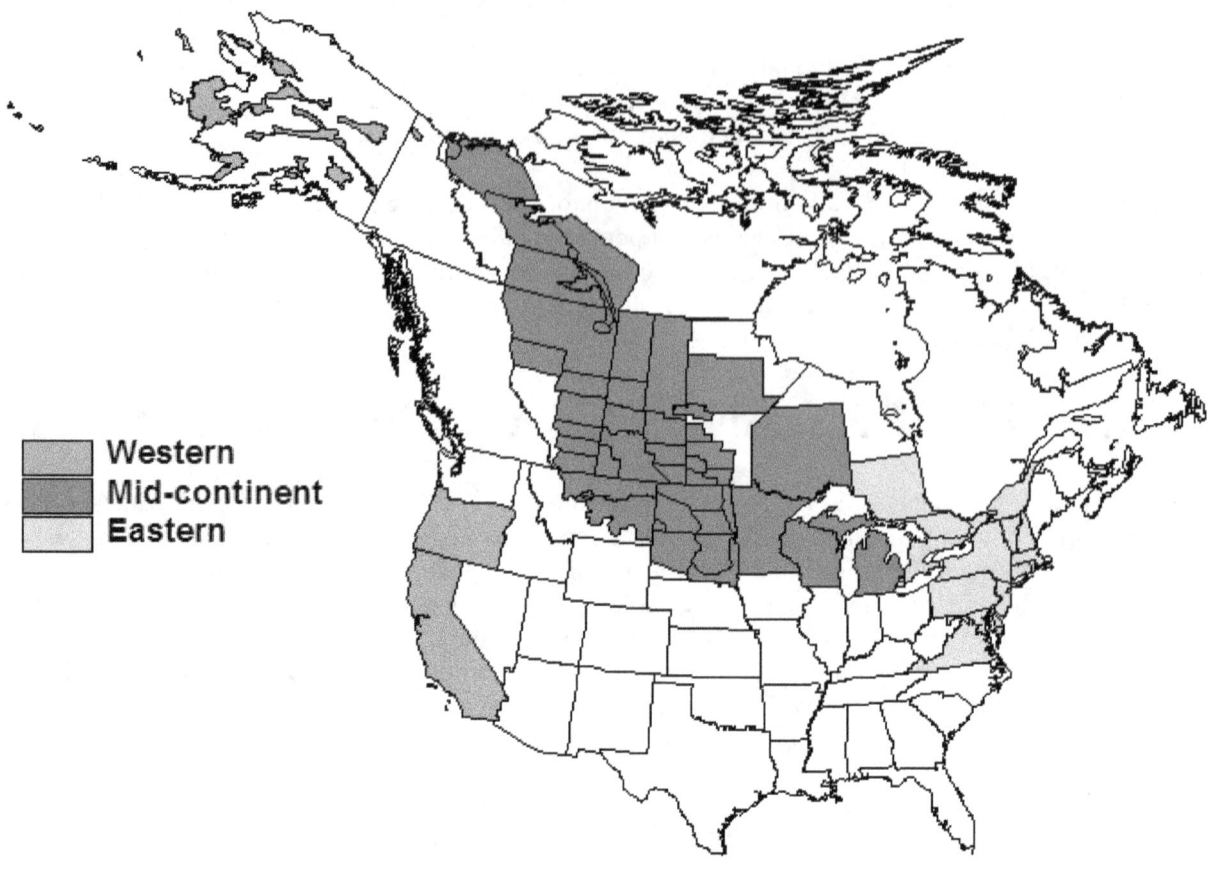

Fig 1. Survey areas currently assigned to the mid-continent, eastern, and western stocks of mallards for the purposes of AHM.

MALLARD POPULATION DYNAMICS

Mid-Continent Stock

For this year, mid-continent mallards have been re-defined as those breeding in WBPHS strata 13–18, 20–50, and 75–77, and in the Great Lakes region (Michigan, Minnesota, and Wisconsin; Fig. 1). Estimates of the size of this population are available since 1992, and have varied from 6.4 to 11.2 million (Table 1, Fig. 2). Estimated breeding-population size in 2008 was 7.87 million (SE = 0.26 million), including 7.19 million (SE = 0.29 million) from the WBPHS and 675 thousand (SE = 48 thousand) from the Great Lakes region.

Details describing the set of population models for mid-continent mallards are provided in Appendix 2. The set consists of four alternatives, formed by the combination of two survival hypotheses (additive vs. compensatory hunting mortality) and two reproductive hypotheses (strongly vs. weakly density dependent). Relative weights for the alternative models of mid-continent mallards changed little until all models under-predicted the change in population size from 1998 to 1999, perhaps indicating there is a significant factor affecting population dynamics that is absent from all four models (Fig. 3). Updated model weights suggest some preference for the additive-

Table 1. Estimates (N) and associated standard errors (SE) of mid-continent mallards (in millions) in the WBPHS (strata 13–18, 20–50, and 75–77) and the Great Lakes region (Michigan, Minnesota, and Wisconsin).

Year	WBPHS area		Great Lakes region		Total	
	N	SE	N	SE	N	SE
1992	5.6304	0.2379	0.9946	0.1597	6.6249	0.2865
1993	5.4253	0.2068	0.9347	0.1457	6.3600	0.2529
1994	6.6292	0.2803	1.1505	0.1163	7.7797	0.3035
1995	7.7452	0.2793	1.1214	0.1965	8.8666	0.3415
1996	7.4193	0.2593	1.0251	0.1443	8.4444	0.2967
1997	9.3554	0.3041	1.0777	0.1445	10.4331	0.3367
1998	8.8041	0.2940	1.1224	0.1792	9.9266	0.3443
1999	10.0926	0.3374	1.0591	0.2122	11.1518	0.3986
2000	8.6999	0.2855	1.2350	0.1761	9.9348	0.3354
2001	7.1857	0.2204	0.8622	0.1086	8.0479	0.2457
2002	6.8364	0.2412	1.0820	0.1152	7.9184	0.2673
2003	7.1062	0.2589	0.8360	0.0734	7.9422	0.2691
2004	6.6142	0.2746	0.9333	0.0748	7.5474	0.2847
2005	6.0521	0.2754	0.7862	0.0650	6.8383	0.2830
2006	6.7607	0.2187	0.5881	0.0465	7.3488	0.2236
2007	7.7258	0.2805	0.7677	0.0584	8.4935	0.2865
2008	7.1914	0.2525	0.6750	0.0478	7.8664	0.2570

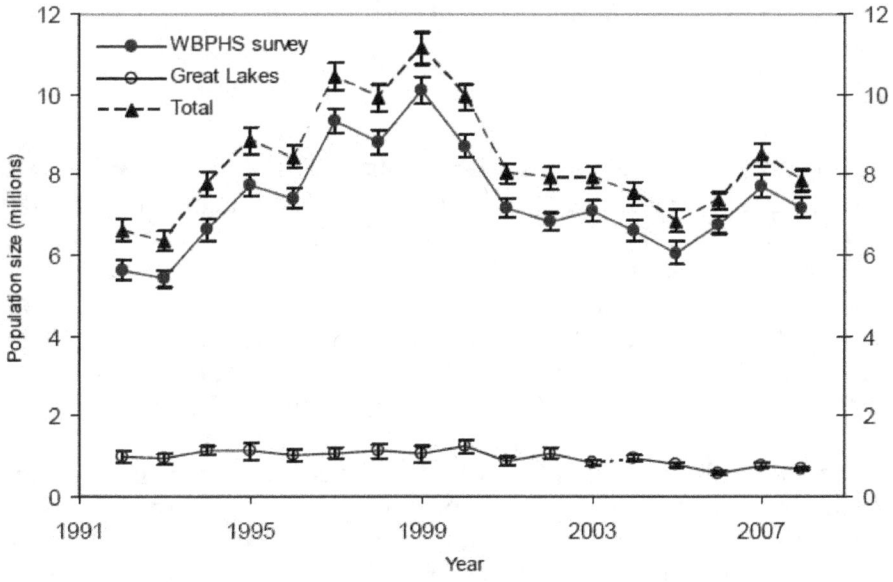

Fig. 2. Population estimates of mid-continent mallards in the WBPHS (strata: 13–18, 20–50, and 75–77) and the Great Lakes region (Michigan, Minnesota, and Wisconsin). Error bars represent one standard error.

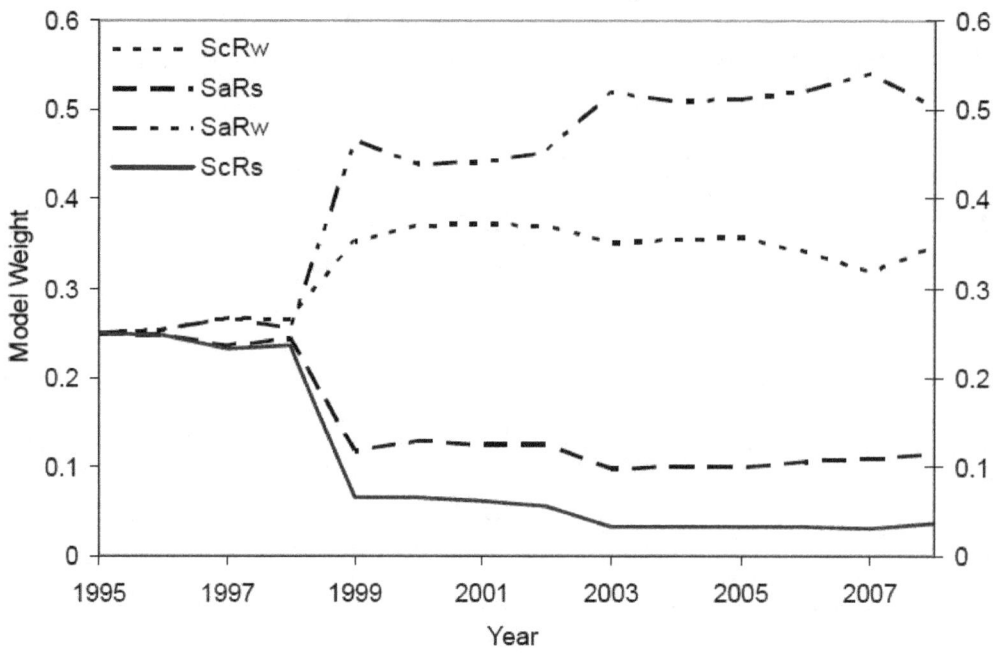

Fig 3. Weights for models of mid-continent mallards (ScRs = compensatory mortality and strongly density-dependent reproduction, ScRw = compensatory mortality and weakly density-dependent reproduction, SaRs = additive mortality and strongly density-dependent reproduction, and SaRw = additive mortality and weakly density-dependent reproduction). Model weights were assumed to be equal in 1995.

mortality models (62%) over those describing hunting mortality as compensatory (38%). For most of the time frame, model weights have strongly favored the weakly density-dependent reproductive models over the strongly density-dependent ones, with current model weights of 85% and 15%, respectively. The reader is cautioned, however, that models can sometimes make reliable predictions of population size for reasons having little to do with the biological hypotheses expressed therein (Johnson et al. 2002b).

Eastern Stock

Eastern mallards are defined as those breeding in southern Ontario and Quebec (WBPHS strata 51–54 and 56) and in the northeastern U.S. (AFBWS; Heusman and Sauer 2000; Fig. 1). Estimates of population size have varied from 815 thousand to 1.1 million since 1990, with the majority of the population accounted for in the northeastern U.S. (Table 2, Fig. 4). For 2008, the estimated breeding-population size of eastern mallards was 815 thousand (SE = 51 thousand), including 619 thousand (SE = 41 thousand) from the northeastern U.S. and 196 thousand (SE = 30 thousand) from the WBPHS. The reader is cautioned that these estimates differ from those reported in the USFWS annual waterfowl trend and status reports, which include composite estimates based on more fixed-wing strata in eastern Canada and helicopter surveys conducted by the Canadian Wildlife Service (CWS).

Details concerning the set of population models for eastern mallards are provided in Appendix 3. The set consists of six alternatives, formed by the combination of two reproductive hypotheses (strongly vs. weakly density dependent) and three hypotheses concerning bias in estimates of survival and reproductive rates (no bias vs. biased survival rates vs. biased reproductive rates). With respect to model weights, there is no single model that is clearly favored over the others at the current time. Collectively, current model weights provide little discrimination between the weakly density-dependent or strongly density dependence reproductive hypotheses, with current model weights of 54% and 46%, respectively (Fig. 5). In addition, there is overwhelming evidence of bias in extant estimates of survival or reproductive rates (100%), assuming that survey estimates are unbiased.

Table 2. Estimates (N) and associated standard errors (SE) of eastern mallards (in thousands) in the northeastern U.S. (AFBWS) and southern Ontario and Quebec (WBPHS strata 51–54 and 56).

	Northeastern U.S.		Canadian survey strata		Total	
Year	N	SE	N	SE	N	SE
1990	665.1	78.3	190.7	47.2	855.8	91.4
1991	779.2	88.3	152.8	33.7	932.0	94.5
1992	562.2	47.9	320.3	53.0	882.5	71.5
1993	686.6	49.9	292.1	48.2	978.6	69.4
1994	856.3	62.8	219.5	28.2	1075.8	68.8
1995	864.1	70.4	184.4	40.0	1048.6	81.0
1996	848.6	61.1	283.1	55.7	1131.7	82.6
1997	795.2	49.6	212.1	39.6	1007.3	63.4
1998	775.2	49.7	263.8	67.2	1039.0	83.6
1999	880.0	60.2	212.5	36.9	1092.4	70.6
2000	762.6	48.7	132.3	26.4	894.8	55.4
2001	809.4	51.6	200.2	35.6	1009.7	62.7
2002	833.5	56.2	191.5	31.9	1025.0	64.7
2003	731.9	47.0	308.3	55.4	1040.2	72.6
2004	806.6	51.7	301.5	53.3	1108.1	74.3
2005	753.6	53.6	293.4	53.1	1047.0	75.5
2006	721.4	47.6	174.0	28.4	895.4	55.5
2007	687.6	46.7	219.3	33.6	906.9	57.6
2008	619.1	40.7	196.0	30.0	815.1	50.5

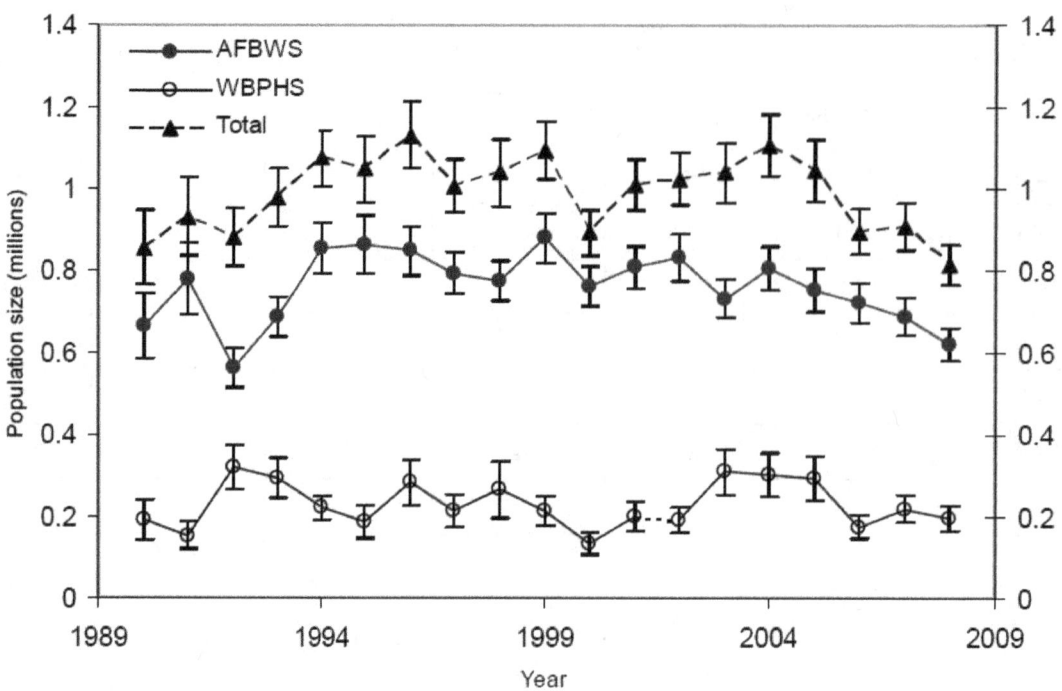

Fig. 4. Population estimates of eastern mallards in the northeastern states (AFBWS) and in southern Ontario and Quebec (WBPHS strata 51–54 and 56). Error bars represent one standard error.

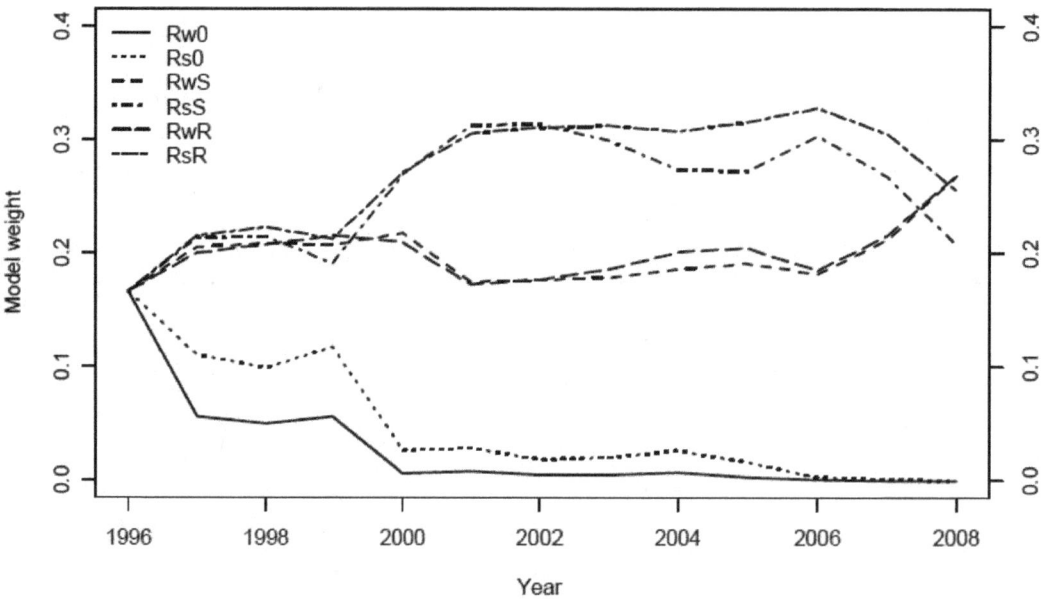

Fig. 5. Weights for models of eastern mallards (Rw0 = weak density-dependent reproduction and no model bias, Rs0 = strong -dependent reproduction and no model bias, RwS = weak density-dependent reproduction and biased survival rates, RsS = strong density-dependent reproduction and biased survival rates, RwR = weak density-dependent reproduction and biased reproductive rates, and RsR = strong density-dependent reproduction and biased reproductive rates). Model weights were assumed to be equal in 1996.

Western Stock

Western mallards consist of 2 substocks and are defined as those birds breeding in Alaska (WBPHS strata 1–12) and those birds breeding in California and Oregon (state surveys). Estimates of the size of these subpopulations have varied from 283 to 843 thousand in Alaska since 1990 and 355 to 694 thousand in California and Oregon since 1992 (Table 3, Fig. 6). The total population size of western mallards has ranged from 0.748 to 1.407 million.

Ideally, the western mallard stock assessment would account for mallards breeding in the states of the Pacific Flyway (including Alaska), British Columbia, and the Yukon Territory. However, we have had continuing concerns about our ability to determine changes in population size based on the collection of surveys conducted independently by Pacific Flyway States and the CWS in British Columbia. These surveys tend to vary in design and intensity, and in some cases lack measures of precision. We reviewed extant surveys to determine their adequacy for supporting a western-mallard AHM protocol and selected Alaska, California, and Oregon for modeling purposes. These three states likely harbor about 75% of the western-mallard breeding population. Nonetheless, this geographic delineation is considered temporary until surveys in other areas can be brought up to similar standards and an adequate record of population estimates is available for analysis.

Details concerning the set of population models for western mallards are provided in Appendix 4. To predict changes in abundance we relied on a discrete logistic model, which combines reproduction and natural mortality into a single parameter, r, the intrinsic rate of growth. This model assumes density-dependent growth, which is regulated by the ratio of population size, N, to the carrying capacity of the environment, K (i.e., equilibrium population size in the absence of harvest). In the traditional formulation of the logistic model, harvest mortality is completely additive and any compensation for hunting losses occurs as a result of density-dependent responses beginning in the subsequent breeding season. To increase the model's generality we included a scaling parameter for harvest that allows for the possibility of compensation prior to the breeding season. It is important to note, however, that this parameterization does not incorporate any hypothesized mechanism for harvest compensation and, therefore, must be interpreted cautiously. We modeled Alaska mallards independently of those in California and Oregon because of differing population trajectories (Fig. 6) and substantial differences in the distribution of band recoveries.

We used Bayesian estimation methods in combination with a state-space model that accounts explicitly for both process and observation error in breeding population size (Meyer and Millar 1999). Breeding population estimates of mallards in Alaska are available since 1955, but we had to limit the time-series to 1990–2005 because of changes in survey methodology and insufficient band-recovery data. The logistic model and associated posterior parameter estimates provided a reasonable fit to the observed time-series of Alaska population estimates. The estimated carrying capacity was 1.2 million, the intrinsic rate of growth was 0.32, and harvest mortality acted in an additive fashion. Breeding population and harvest-rate data were available for California-Oregon mallards for the period 1992–2006. The logistic model also provided a reasonable fit to these data, suggesting a carrying capacity of 0.7 million, an intrinsic rate of growth of 0.36, and harvest mortality that acted in only a partially additive manner.

Table 3. Estimates (N) and associated standard errors (SE) of mallards (in thousands) in Alaska (WBPHS strata 1–12) and California and Oregon (state surveys) combined.

	Alaska		California-Oregon		Total	
Year	N	SE	N	SE	N	SE
1990	366.9	37.0				
1991	385.3	36.3				
1992	345.7	38.7	483.5	60.5	829.2	71.8
1993	283.0	29.5	465.4	51.0	748.4	58.9
1994	350.9	37.1	436.7	42.6	787.6	56.5
1995	524.2	68.0	454.1	42.8	978.3	80.3
1996	522.0	43.6	645.1	80.2	1167.1	91.2
1997	584.2	52.0	639.0	104.3	1223.2	116.6
1998	836.2	67.3	486.8	48.9	1323.0	83.2
1999	713.1	69.6	693.7	106.6	1406.8	127.3
2000	770.3	52.2	463.9	53.2	1234.2	74.5
2001	718.3	54.1	404.4	45.1	1122.7	70.5
2002	667.3	50.7	377.5	32.7	1044.9	60.3
2003	843.5	66.8	434.0	50.1	1277.5	83.5
2004	811.1	63.9	354.7	35.2	1165.8	72.9
2005	703.1	54.7	401.4	47.4	1104.5	72.4
2006	515.8	46.9	487.9	57.6	1003.7	74.3
2007	581.5	55.1	490.0	54.6	1071.5	77.5
2008	532.4	46.8	381.4	47.8	913.8	66.9

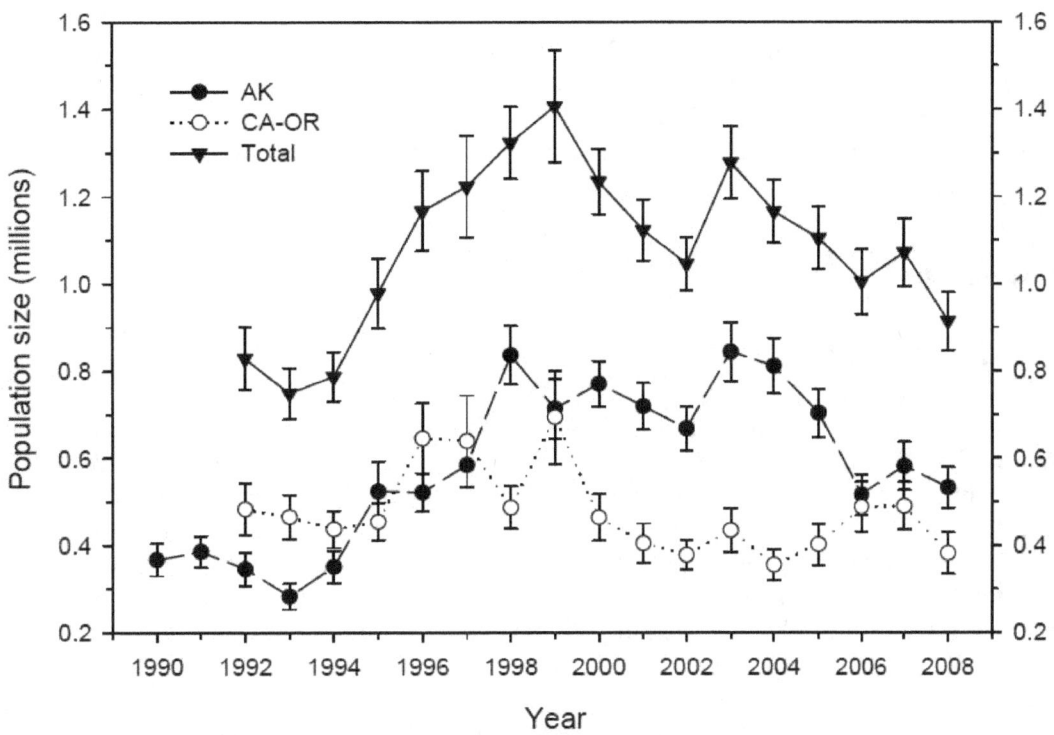

Fig. 6. Population estimates of western mallards in Alaska (WBPHS strata 1–12) and California and Oregon (state surveys) combined. Error bars represent one standard error.

Ideally, the development of AHM protocols for mallards would consider how different breeding stocks distribute themselves among the four flyways so that Flyway-specific harvest strategies could account for the mixing of birds during the hunting season. At present, however, a joint optimization of western, mid-continent, and eastern stocks is not feasible due to computational hurdles. However, our preliminary analyses suggest that the lack of a joint optimization does not result in a significant decrease in performance. Therefore, the AHM protocol for western mallards is structured similarly to that used for eastern mallards, in which an optimal harvest strategy is based on the status of a single breeding stock and harvest regulations in a single flyway. Although the contribution of mid-continent mallards to the Pacific Flyway harvest is significant, we believe an independent harvest strategy for western mallards poses little risk to the mid-continent stock. Further analyses will be needed to confirm this conclusion, as well as to better understand the potential effect of mid-continent mallard status on sustainable hunting opportunities in the Pacific Flyway.

HARVEST-MANAGEMENT OBJECTIVES

The basic harvest-management objective for mid-continent mallards is to maximize cumulative harvest over the long term, which inherently requires perpetuation of a viable population. Moreover, this objective is constrained to avoid regulations that could be expected to result in a subsequent population size below the goal of the North American Waterfowl Management Plan (NAWMP). According to this constraint, the value of harvest decreases proportionally as the difference between the goal and expected population size increases. This balance of harvest and population objectives results in a regulatory strategy that is more conservative than that for maximizing long-term harvest, but more liberal than a strategy to attain the NAWMP goal (regardless of effects on hunting opportunity). The current objective uses a population goal of 8.5 million mallards, which is based on 7.9 million mallards from the WBPHS (strata 13–18, 20–50, and 75–77) based on the 1998 update of the NAWMP and a goal of 0.6 million for the combined states of Michigan, Minnesota, and Wisconsin.

For eastern and western mallards, there is no NAWMP goal or other established target for desired population size. Accordingly, the management objective for eastern and western mallards is simply to maximize long-term cumulative (i.e., sustainable) harvest. Additionally for western mallards, maximum long-term cumulative harvest is subject to a constraint intended to prevent extreme changes in regulations associated with relatively small changes in population sizes.

REGULATORY ALTERNATIVES

Evolution of Alternatives

When AHM was first implemented in 1995, three regulatory alternatives characterized as liberal, moderate, and restrictive were defined based on regulations used during 1979–84, 1985–87, and 1988–93, respectively. These regulatory alternatives also were considered for the 1996 hunting season. In 1997, the regulatory alternatives were modified to include: (1) the addition of a very-restrictive alternative; (2) additional days and a higher duck bag limit in the moderate and liberal alternatives; and (3) an increase in the bag limit of hen mallards in the moderate and liberal alternatives. In 2002 the USFWS further modified the moderate and liberal alternatives to include extensions of approximately one week in both the opening and closing framework dates.

In 2003 the very-restrictive alternative was eliminated at the request of the Flyway Councils. Expected harvest rates under the very-restrictive alternative did not differ significantly from those under the restrictive alternative, and the very-restrictive alternative was expected to be prescribed for < 5% of all hunting seasons. Also in 2003, at the request of the Flyway Councils the USFWS agreed to exclude closed duck-hunting seasons from the AHM protocol when the population size of mid-continent mallards was ≥ 5.5 million (WBPHS strata 1–18, 20–50, and 75–77 plus the Great Lakes region). Based on our original assessment, closed hunting seasons did not appear to be necessary from the perspective of sustainable harvesting when the mid-continent mallard population exceeded this level. The impact of maintaining open seasons above this level also appeared negligible for other mid-continent duck species, as based on population models developed by Johnson (2003).

This year, based on the re-definition of the mid-continent mallard stock that excludes mallards breeding in Alaska, we re-scaled the closed-season constraint. Initially, we attempted to adjust the original 5.5 million closure threshold by subtracting out the 1985 Alaska breeding population estimate, which was the year upon which the original closed season constraint was based. Our initial re-scaling resulted in a new threshold equal to 5.25 million. Simulations based on optimal policies using this revised closed season constraint suggested that the Mississippi and Central Flyways would experience a 70% increase in the frequency of closed seasons. At this time, we agreed to consider alternative re-scalings in order to minimize the effects on the mid-continent mallard strategy and account for the increase in mean breeding population sizes in Alaska over the past several decades. Based on this assessment, we recommended a revised closed season constraint of 4.75 million which resulted in a strategy performance equivalent to the performance expected prior to the re-definition of the mid-continent mallard stock. Because the performance of the revised strategy is essentially unchanged from the original strategy, we believe it will have no greater impact on other duck stocks in the Mississippi and Central Flyways. However, complete or partial season-closures for particular species or populations could still be deemed necessary in some situations regardless of the status of mid-continent mallards. Details of the regulatory alternatives for each Flyway are provided in Table 4.

Table 4. Regulatory alternatives for the 2008 duck-hunting season.

Regulation	Flyway			
	Atlantic[a]	Mississippi	Central[b]	Pacific[c]
Shooting hours	one-half hour before sunrise to sunset			
Framework dates				
Restrictive	Oct 1 – Jan 20	Saturday nearest Oct 1to the Sunday nearest Jan 20		
Moderate and Liberal	Saturday nearest September 24 to the last Sunday in January			
Season length (days)				
Restrictive	30	30	39	60
Moderate	45	45	60	86
Liberal	60	60	74	107
Bag limit (total / mallard / female mallard)				
Restrictive	3 / 3 / 1	3 / 2 / 1	3 / 3 / 1	4 / 3 / 1
Moderate	6 / 4 / 2	6 / 4 / 1	6 / 5 / 1	7 / 5 / 2
Liberal	6 / 4 / 2	6 / 4 / 2	6 / 5 / 2	7 / 7 / 2

[a] The states of Maine, Massachusetts, Connecticut, Pennsylvania, New Jersey, Maryland, Delaware, West Virginia, Virginia, and North Carolina are permitted to exclude Sundays, which are closed to hunting, from their total allotment of season days.
[b] The High Plains Mallard Management Unit is allowed 12, 23, and 23 extra days in the restrictive, moderate, and liberal alternatives, respectively.
[c] The Columbia Basin Mallard Management Unit is allowed seven extra days in the restrictive, and moderate alternatives.

Regulation-Specific Harvest Rates

Harvest rates of mallards associated with each of the open-season regulatory alternatives were initially predicted using harvest-rate estimates from 1979–84, which were adjusted to reflect current hunter numbers and contemporary specifications of season lengths and bag limits. In the case of closed seasons in the U.S., we assumed rates of harvest would be similar to those observed in Canada during 1988–93, which was a period of restrictive regulations both in Canada and the U.S. All harvest-rate predictions were based only in part on band-recovery data, and relied heavily on models of hunting effort and success derived from hunter surveys (Appendix C in USFWS 2002). As such, these predictions had large sampling variances and their accuracy was uncertain.

In 2002, we began relying on Bayesian statistical methods for improving regulation-specific predictions of harvest rates, including predictions of the effects of framework-date extensions. Essentially, the idea is to use existing (prior) information to develop initial harvest-rate predictions (as above), to make regulatory decisions based on those predictions, and then to observe realized harvest rates. Those observed harvest rates, in turn, are treated as new sources of information for calculating updated (posterior) predictions. Bayesian methods are attractive because they provide a quantitative and formal, yet intuitive, approach to adaptive management.

For mid-continent mallards, we have empirical estimates of harvest rate from the recent period of liberal hunting regulations (1998–2007). The Bayesian methods thus allow us to combine these estimates with our prior predictions to provide updated estimates of harvest rates expected under the liberal regulatory alternative. Moreover, in the absence of experience (so far) with the restrictive and moderate regulatory alternatives, we reasoned that our initial predictions of harvest rates associated with those alternatives should be re-scaled based on a comparison of predicted and observed harvest rates under the liberal regulatory alternative. In other words, if observed harvest rates under the liberal alternative were 10% less than predicted, then we might also expect that the mean harvest rate under the moderate alternative would be 10% less than predicted. The appropriate scaling factors currently are based exclusively on prior beliefs about differences in mean harvest rate among regulatory alternatives, but they will be updated once we have experience with something other than the liberal alternative. A detailed description of the analytical framework for modeling mallard harvest rates is provided in Appendix 5.

Our models of regulation-specific harvest rates also allow for the marginal effect of framework-date extensions in the moderate and liberal alternatives. A previous analysis by the USFWS (2001) suggested that implementation of framework-date extensions might be expected to increase the harvest rate of mid-continent mallards by about 15%, or in absolute terms by about 0.02 (SD = 0.01). Based on the observed harvest rates during the 2002–2007 hunting seasons, the updated (posterior) estimate of the marginal change in harvest rate attributable to the framework-date extension is 0.006 (SD = 0.008). The estimated effect of the framework-date extension has been to increase harvest rate of mid-continent mallards by about 5% over what would otherwise be expected in the liberal alternative. However, the reader is strongly cautioned that reliable inference about the marginal effect of framework-date extensions ultimately depends on a rigorous experimental design (including controls and random application of treatments).

Current predictions of harvest rates of adult-male mid-continent mallards associated with each of the regulatory alternatives are provided in Table 5. Predictions of harvest rates for the other age-sex cohorts are based on the historical ratios of cohort-specific harvest rates to adult-male rates (Runge et al. 2002). These ratios are considered fixed at their long-term averages and are 1.5407, 0.7191, and 1.1175 for young males, adult females, and young females, respectively. We make the simplifying assumption that the harvest rates of mid-continent mallards depend solely on the regulatory choice in the Mississippi and Central Flyways.

Table 5. Predictions of harvest rates of adult-male mid-continent mallards expected with application of the 2008 regulatory alternatives in the Mississippi and Central Flyways.

Regulatory alternative	Mean	SD
Closed (U.S.)	0.0088	0.0019
Restrictive	0.0560	0.0129
Moderate	0.0978	0.0216
Liberal	0.1153	0.0207

The predicted harvest rates of eastern-mallard are updated in the same fashion as that for mid-continent mallards based on reward banding conducted in eastern Canada and the northeastern U.S. (Appendix 5). Like mid-continent mallards, harvest rates of age and sex cohorts other than adult male mallards are based on constant rates of differential vulnerability as derived from band-recovery data. For eastern mallards, these constants are 1.153, 1.331, and 1.509 for adult females, young males, and young females, respectively (Johnson et al. 2002a). Regulation-specific predictions of harvest rates of adult-male eastern mallards are provided in Table 6.

In contrast to mid-continent mallards, framework-date extensions were expected to increase the harvest rate of eastern mallards by only about 5% (USFWS 2001), or in absolute terms by about 0.01 (SD = 0.01). Based on the observed harvest rates during the 2002–2007 hunting seasons, the updated (posterior) estimate of the marginal change in harvest rate attributable to the framework-date extension is 0.004 (SD = 0.010). The estimated effect of the framework-date extension has been to increase harvest rate of eastern mallards by about 3% over what would otherwise be expected in the liberal alternative.

Table 6. Predictions of harvest rates of adult-male eastern mallards expected with application of the 2008 regulatory alternatives in the Atlantic Flyway.

Regulatory alternative	Mean	SD
Closed (U.S.)	0.0789	0.0233
Restrictive	0.1126	0.0394
Moderate	0.1407	0.0471
Liberal	0.1528	0.0446

Based on available estimates of harvest rates of mallards banded in California and Oregon during 1990–1995 and 2002–2007, there is no apparent relationship between harvest rate and regulatory changes in the Pacific Flyway. This is unusual given our ability to document such a relationship in other mallard stocks and in other species. We note, however, that the period 2002–2007 was comprised of both stable and liberal regulations and harvest rate estimates were based solely on reward bands. Regulations were relatively restrictive during most of the earlier period and harvest rates were estimated based on standard bands using reporting rates estimated from reward banding during 1987–1988. Additionally, 1993–1995 were transition years in which full-address and toll-free bands were being introduced and information to assess their reporting rates (and their effects on reporting rates of standard bands) is limited. Thus, the two periods in which we wish to compare harvest rates are characterized not only by changes in regulations, but also in estimation methods.

Consequently, we lack a sound empirical basis for predicting harvest rates of western mallards associated with current regulatory alternatives in the Pacific Flyway. For this year, however, we specified regulation-specific harvest rates with associated standard deviations for the closed, restrictive, moderate, and liberal alternatives (Table 7). Harvest rates for the liberal alternative were based on empirical estimates realized under the current liberal alternative during 2002–2007 and determined from adult-male mallards banded with reward bands in California and Oregon. Harvest rates for the moderate and restrictive alternatives were based on the proportional (0.85 and 0.51) difference in harvest rates expected for mid-continent mallards under the respective alternatives. A relatively large standard deviation (CV=0.3) was chosen to reflect greater uncertainty about the means than that for mid-continent mallards (CV=0.2). And finally, harvest rate for the closed alternative was based on what we might realize with a closed season in the U.S. (including Alaska) and a very restrictive season in Canada, similar to that for mid-continent mallards. Prior to next year, assumptions about harvest rates will be reviewed and modified if appropriate. Further, we intend to develop a Bayesian hierarchical framework to update harvest rate estimates as experience allows. This framework will be analogous to that currently in use for mid-continent and eastern mallards (refer to Appendix 5).

Table 7. Predictions of harvest rates of adult-male western mallards expected with application of the 2008 regulatory alternatives in the Atlantic Flyway.

Regulatory alternative	Mean	SD
Closed (U.S.)	0.110	0.010
Restrictive	0.090	0.030
Moderate	0.060	0.020
Liberal	0.001	0.002

OPTIMAL REGULATORY STRATEGIES

We calculated optimal regulatory strategies using stochastic dynamic programming (Lubow 1995, Johnson and Williams 1999). For the Mississippi and Central Flyways, we based this optimization on: (1) the 2008 regulatory alternatives, including the closed-season constraint; (2) current population models and associated weights for mid-continent mallards; and (3) the dual objectives of maximizing long-term cumulative harvest and achieving a population goal of 8.5 million mid-continent mallards. The resulting regulatory strategy reflects the changes resulting from the removal of Alaska from the mid-continent stock (Table 8). Note that prescriptions for closed seasons in this strategy represent resource conditions that are insufficient to support one of the current regulatory alternatives, given current harvest-management objectives and constraints. However, closed seasons under all of these conditions are not necessarily required for long-term resource protection, and simply reflect the NAWMP population goal and the nature of the current regulatory alternatives. Assuming that regulatory choices adhered to this strategy (and that current model weights accurately reflect population dynamics), breeding-population size would be expected to average 6.82 million (SD = 1.83 million). Based on an estimated population size of 7.87 million mid-continent mallards and 3.05 million ponds in Prairie Canada, the optimal choice for the Mississippi and Central Flyways in 2008 is the liberal regulatory alternative.

We calculated an optimal regulatory strategy for the Atlantic Flyway based on: (1) the 2008 regulatory alternatives; (2) current population models and associated weights for eastern mallards; and (3) an objective to maximize long-term cumulative harvest. The resulting strategy suggests liberal regulations for all population sizes of record, and is characterized by a lack of intermediate regulations (Table 9). We simulated the use of this regulatory strategy to determine expected performance characteristics. Assuming that harvest management adhered to this strategy (and that current model weights accurately reflect population dynamics), breeding-population size would be expected to average 891 thousand (SD = 17 thousand). Based on an estimated breeding population size of 815 thousand mallards, the optimal choice for the Atlantic Flyway in 2008 is the liberal regulatory alternative.

We calculated an optimal regulatory strategy for the Pacific Flyway based on: (1) the 2008 regulatory alternatives, (2) current (1990–2007) population models and parameter estimates, and (3) an objective to maximize long-term cumulative harvest subject to a constraint intended to prevent extreme changes in regulations associated with relatively small changes in population sizes (Table 10). We simulated the use of this regulatory strategy to determine expected performance characteristics. Assuming that harvest management adhered to this strategy (and that current model parameters accurately reflect population dynamics), breeding-population size would be expected to average 1.1 million (SD = 0.21 million) in Alaska and 0.48 million (SD = 0.03 million) in California and Oregon. Based on an estimated breeding population size of 532 thousand mallards in Alaska and 381 thousand in California and Oregon, the optimal choice for the Pacific Flyway in 2008 is the liberal regulatory alternative (see Table 10).

Table 8. Optimal regulatory strategy[a] for the Mississippi and Central Flyways for the 2008 hunting season. This strategy is based on current regulatory alternatives (including the closed-season constraint), on current mid-continent mallard models and weights, and on the dual objectives of maximizing long-term cumulative harvest and achieving a population goal of 8.5 million mallards. The shaded cell indicates the regulatory prescription for 2008.

Bpop[b]	Ponds[c]									
	1.5	2.0	2.5	3.0	3.5	4.0	4.5	5.0	5.5	6.0
≤ 4.5	C	C	C	C	C	C	C	C	C	C
4.75–5.50	R	R	R	R	R	R	R	R	R	R
5.75	R	R	R	R	R	R	R	R	R	M
6.00	R	R	R	R	R	R	R	M	L	L
6.25	R	R	R	R	M	M	M	L	L	L
6.50	R	R	R	M	M	L	L	L	L	L
6.75	R	M	M	L	L	L	L	L	L	L
7.00	M	M	L	L	L	L	L	L	L	L
≥ 7.25	L	L	L	L	L	L	L	L	L	L

[a] C = closed season, R = restrictive, M = moderate, L = liberal.
[b] Mallard breeding population size (in millions) in the WBPHS (strata 13–18, 20–50, 75–77) and Michigan, Minnesota, and Wisconsin.
[c] Ponds (in millions) in Prairie Canada in May.

Table 9. Optimal regulatory strategy[a] for the Atlantic Flyway for the 2008 hunting season. This strategy is based on current regulatory alternatives, on current eastern mallard models and weights, and on an objective to maximize long-term cumulative harvest. The shaded cell indicates the regulatory prescription for 2008.

Mallards[b]	Regulation
≤ 250	C
300	R
≥ 350	L

[a] C = closed season, R = restrictive, M = moderate, and L = liberal.
[b] Estimated number of mallards in eastern Canada (WBPHS strata 51–54, 56) and the northeastern U.S. (AFBWS), in thousands.

Table 10. Optimal regulatory strategy[a] for the Pacific Flyway during the 2008 hunting season. This strategy is based on the 2008 regulatory alternatives, current (1990–07) population models and parameter estimates, and an objective to maximize long-term cumulative harvest subject to a constraint intended to prevent extreme changes in regulations associated with relatively small changes in population sizes. The shaded cell indicates the regulatory prescription for 2008.

CA-OR BPOP[b]	Alaska BPOP[b]											
	0	0.05	0.10	0.15	0.20	0.25	0.30	0.35	0.40	0.45	0.50	≥ 0.55
0	C	C	L	L	L	L	L	L	L	L	L	L
0.05	C	C	R	R	R	R	R	R	M	L	L	L
0.10	C	R	R	R	R	R	R	M	L	L	L	L
0.15	R	R	R	R	R	M	L	L	L	L	L	L
0.20	R	R	R	R	M	L	L	L	L	L	L	L
0.25	R	R	M	M	L	L	L	L	L	L	L	L
0.30	M	L	L	L	L	L	L	L	L	L	L	L
0.35	L	L	L	L	L	L	L	L	L	L	L	L
0.40	L	L	L	L	L	L	L	L	L	L	L	L
≥ 0.45	L	L	L	L	L	L	L	L	L	L	L	L

[a] C = closed season, R = restrictive, M = moderate, and L = liberal.
[b] Estimated number of mallards in millions for Alaska (WBPHS strata 1–12) and in California and Oregon.

Application of AHM Concepts to Other Stocks

The USFWS is striving to apply the principles and tools of AHM to improve decision-making for several other stocks of waterfowl. We report on four such efforts in which progress has been made since last year.

American Black Ducks

Beginning in 2003, the USFWS Division of Migratory Bird Management (DMBM) began investigating optimal harvest strategies for black ducks based on models of population dynamics provided by Conroy et al. (2002). As a result of that investigation DMBM concluded that recent harvest rates of black ducks have sometimes been at or above levels consistent with an objective to maximize sustainable harvest. That conclusion ultimately led to a DMBM recommendation in January 2006 to reduce the harvest rate of adult black ducks by 25%. However, the recommendation was subsequently withdrawn because of: (1) published information suggesting that the mid-winter inventory (MWI) may be "capturing" a smaller proportion of the black duck population than in the past (Link et al. 2006); (2) concern about the U.S. acting unilaterally without the benefit of consultation with the CWS; and (3) the short amount of time available to communicate to the public the rationale and nature of restrictions on hunting opportunity.

In November 2006 the international Black Duck Adaptive Harvest Management Working Group (BDAHMWG) met to discuss the most recent analysis by Drs. Mike Conroy and Jon Runge of the Georgia Cooperative Fish and Wildlife Research Unit. Their update of the original analysis by Conroy et al. (2002) suggests that black duck productivity has continued to decline for reasons that cannot be explained by changes in abundance of black ducks (through density dependence) or sympatric mallards (through inter-species competition). However, there were other differences in inferences based on the original and updated analyses that could not be reconciled. The focus of research has now turned to population models based on integrated fixed-wing and helicopter surveys

20

conducted during the breeding season. For the present, however, the question of whether current harvest rates of black ducks are consistent with black duck harvest potential and management objectives remains unanswered.

In 2006, due to potential changes in the wintering distribution of black ducks, the BDAHMWG did not endorse a state-dependent harvest strategy (i.e., one in which optimal harvest rates depend on annual black duck abundance) based on the MWI. However, it was suggested that a constant harvest-rate strategy may perform nearly as well and might provide a basis for a joint Canada-U.S. harvest strategy until an assessment based on integrated breeding-season surveys can be completed. The BDAHMWG agreed to investigate the performance of constant harvest-rate strategies based on the original work of Conroy et al. (2002), recognizing that the original analysis was conducted prior to what may be significant changes in the wintering distribution of black ducks. Thus, it was agreed that the assessment by Conroy et al. (2002) might still provide a reasonable basis for investigating harvest impacts and for evaluating the expected performance of constant harvest-rate strategies. Working within this framework, the BDAHMWG developed a harvest strategy for consideration during the summer of 2007. Negotiations among the CWS, USFWS, Atlantic Flyway, and Mississippi Flyway regarding this harvest strategy failed to reach consensus on several critical issues, namely the specification of an appropriate harvest management objective and on a mechanism for allocating black duck harvest among the U.S. and Canada. In 2007, the USFWS and CWS agreed to provide a forum through which these outstanding issues could be debated and addressed. This led to the formation of the Black Duck International Management Group. This committee consists of policy makers from the CWS, USFWS, Atlantic Flyway, and Mississippi Flyway.

In February 2008, the Black Duck International Management Group met in Ottawa, Ontario to address these and other issues, to review progress on development of a fully adaptive harvest strategy based on integrated breeding population estimates, and to outline the elements of an interim harvest strategy that would be in place until the fully derived strategy is available. At this meeting, the Management Group reached agreement on an interim, prescribed international harvest strategy. This strategy was discussed by the Atlantic and Mississippi Flyways during their winter meetings. Recommendations from these meetings were considered by the Management Group who incorporated many of them into the final proposed interim harvest strategy. The final strategy was endorsed by the USFWS in June 2008 and will be used to guide harvest management decisions in the U.S. and Canada for 3 years unless a fully adaptive protocol is proposed and endorsed by both nations before the end of the 3-year period. If, at the end of 3 years, a fully adaptive strategy is not ready for implementation, the Management Group will review the interim strategy for possible revision and/or extension.

Presently, Dr. Mike Conroy of the Georgia Fish and Wildlife Cooperative Research Unit is developing a revised set of models and a revised adaptive decision framework for black ducks based on integrated breeding population survey estimates. The Black Duck International Management Group is coordinating with Dr. Conroy to ensure that he has all required policy guidance (e.g., agreed upon management objective and constraints, agreed upon harvest allocation rules) to complete development of the decision framework.

Atlantic Population of Canada Geese

For the purposes of this AHM application, Atlantic Population Canada Geese (APCG) are defined as those geese breeding on the Ungava Peninsula. By this delineation, we assume that geese in the Atlantic population outside this area are either few in number, similar in population dynamics to the Ungava birds, or both.

To account for heterogeneity among individuals, we developed a base model consisting of a truncated time-invariant age-based projection model to describe the dynamics of APCG:

$$\mathbf{n}(t+1) = \mathbf{An}(t),$$

where $\mathbf{n}(t)$ is a vector of the abundances of the ages in the population at time t, and $\mathbf{A}$ is the population projection matrix, whose ijth entry a_{ij} gives the contribution of an individual in stage j to stage i over 1 time step. The

projection t to $t+1$ is with the taken in mid-model has a census). The diagram transition

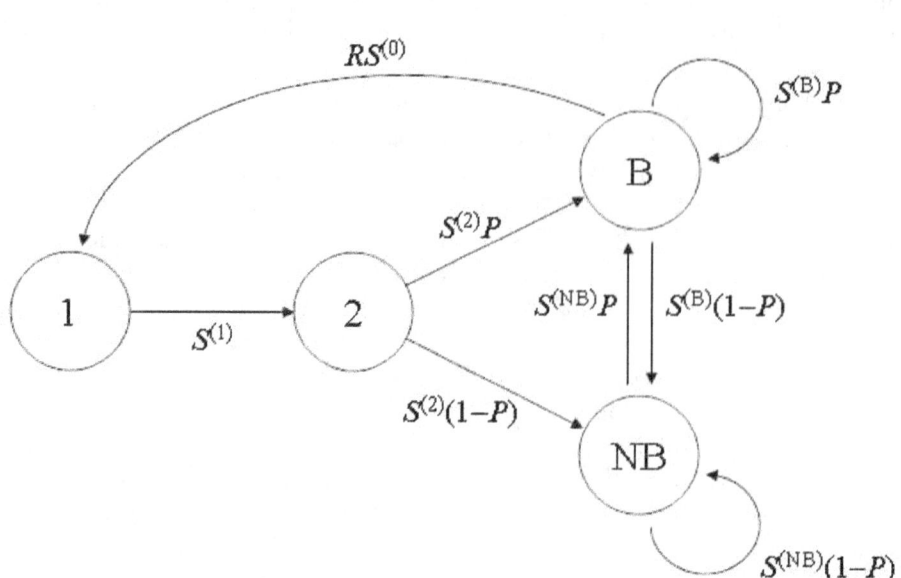

interval (from one year, census being June (i.e., this pre-breeding life cycle reflecting the sequence is:

where node 1 refers to one-year-old birds ($N^{(1)}$), node 2 refers to two-year-old birds ($N^{(2)}$), node B refers to adult breeders ($N^{(B)}$), and node NB refers to adult non-breeders $N^{(NB)}$. One immediate extension of the base model is to remove the assumption of time-invariance, and express the parameters as time-dependent quantities:

P_t = proportion of adult birds in population in year t which breed;

R_t = basic breeding productivity in year t (per capita);

$S_t^{(0)}$ = annual survival rate of young from fledging in year t to the census point the next year;

$S_t^{(1)}$ = annual survival rate of one-year-old birds in year t; etc.

For APCG, only $N^{(B)}$, R and z are observable annually, where $N^{(B)}$ is the number of breeding adults, R is the per capita reproductive rate (ratio of fledged young to breeding adults), and z is an extrinsic, environmental variable (a function of timing of snow melt on the breeding grounds) that is used to predict R.

Note that at the time of the management decision in the United States (July), estimates for only the breeding population size and the environmental variable(s) are available; the age-ratio isn't estimated until later in the summer. Thus, in year t, the observable state variables are $N_t^{(B)}$, z_t, and R_{t-1}.

There are several other state variables of interest, however, namely, $N^{(1)}$, $N^{(2)}$, and $N^{(NB)}$. Because annual harvest decisions need to be made based on the total population size (N^{tot}), which is the sum of contributions from various non-breeding age classes as well as the number of breeding individuals, abundance of non-breeding individuals

$(N^{(NB)}, N^{(1)},$ and $N^{(2)})$ needs to be derived using population-reconstruction techniques. In most cases, population reconstruction involves estimating the most likely population projection matrix, given a time series of population vectors (where number of individuals in each age class at each time is known). However, in our case, only estimates of N^B, R and z are available (not the complete population vector); in effect, we must estimate some of the population abundance values given the other parameters in the model. We developed a fully integrated Bayesian hierarchical model to reconstruct goose population dynamics and formally estimate the unobserved population parameters. With this approach, the survival, recruitment, and reconstruction analyses are embedded into a common estimation platform that allows us to estimate the age structure of the population while simultaneously accounting for all forms of sampling uncertainty.

The time series of breeding population size, age-ratio, and band recovery data were used to reconstruct the population structure from 1997 to 2007, using a density-independent model (Fig. 7A). The estimated population structure in 2007 is: 369.5 thousand breeding adults, 70.3 thousand non-breeding adults, 270.8 thousand second-year birds, and 357.9 thousand first-year birds (Fig. 7B). The density-independent model projects significant increases in the number of breeding pairs (~25% over the next two years) as these two sizeable cohorts come of age.

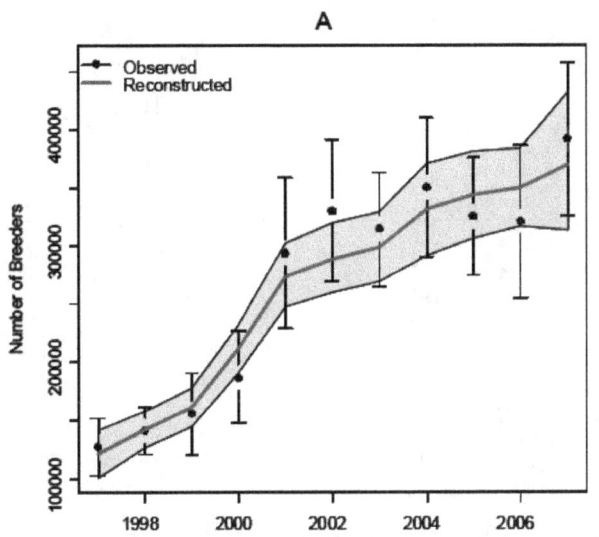 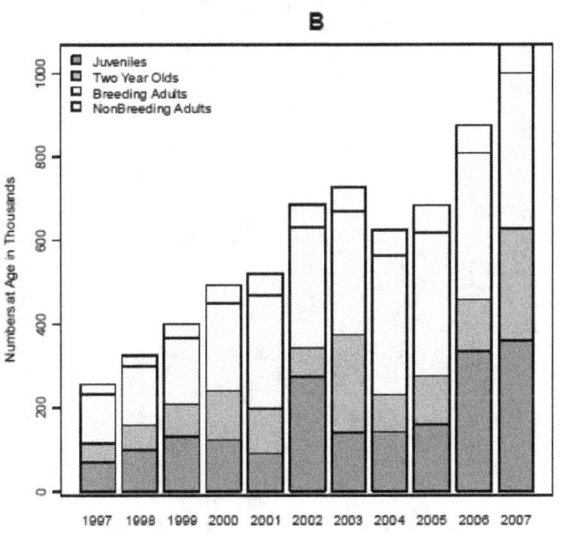

Fig. 7. A. APCG breeding population size (in thousands), 1997–2007, with fitted values from reconstruction (Model 1: density-independent). The closed circles show the observed estimates of breeding population size (not breeding pairs); errors bars are ±2 SE. The solid line shows the breeding population size estimated from the population reconstruction (gray shading represents the 95% credibility interval). B. The age structure of the reconstructed population.

We require a way to forecast changes in population sizes as a function of the current population structure, the intended harvest rate, and the observed weather variables. We have begun developing 4 alternative models to capture the key uncertainties in our ability to predict population changes. These models include density-independent population growth, density-dependent survival, density-dependent breeding propensity, and reporting bias. We will parameterize these models with the integrated modeling framework while also estimating the process variance.

An example harvest strategy for the density-independent model is shown in Fig. 8. The strategy suggests a closed season under the 2007 population and environmental conditions, in order to increase more quickly toward the desired population size. Note that the recommended harvest rate is not strongly affected by the measure of current environmental conditions on the breeding grounds. The policy is very sensitive to the number of breeding adults and second-year birds, while harvest recommendations are strongly affected by uncertainty about the underlying population dynamics. We are starting to develop methods to weight the alternative models and produce a composite optimal policy; such development is a high priority. In addition, we are in the process of fitting the projection models to develop the model set and have begun exploring how to soften the knife-edge property of the policy by including a cost function in the optimization.

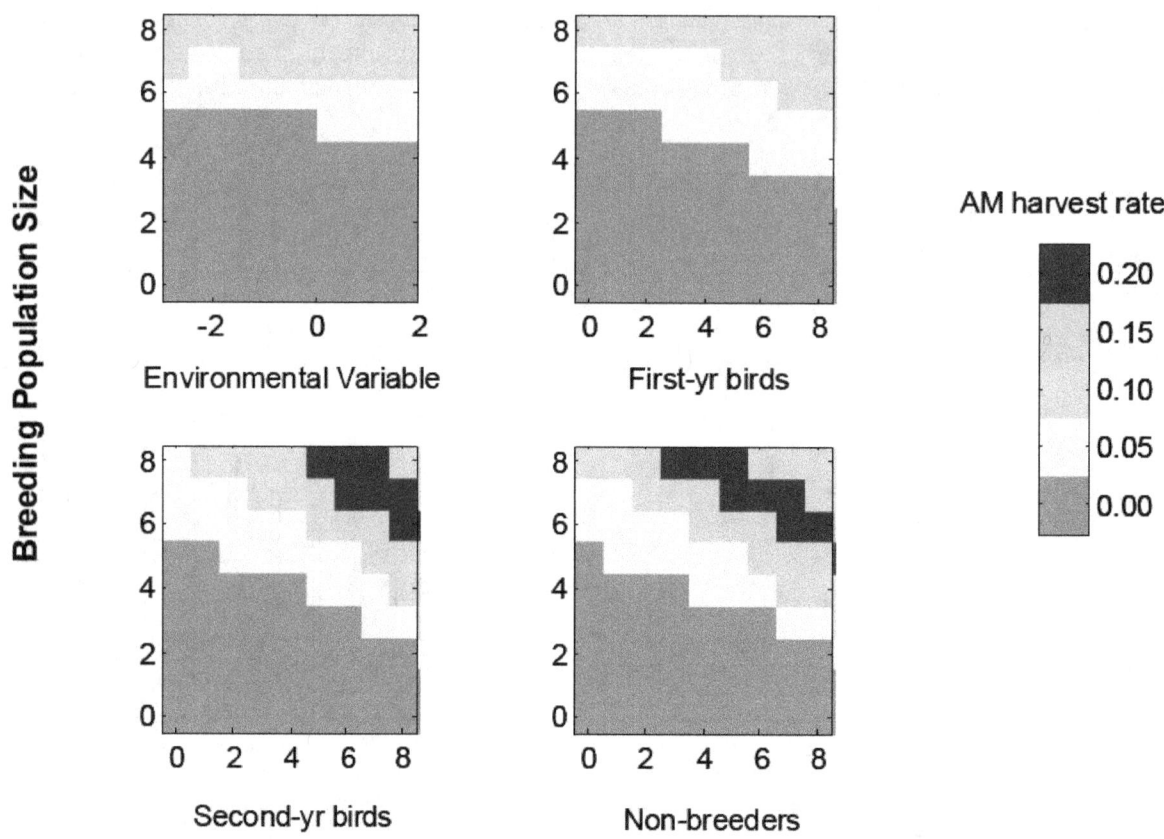

Fig. 8. Examples of optimal harvest strategies for 2007 for models 1 (density-independent). These matrices show the breeding population size against the measure of breeding habitat conditions (principal component of the weather variables), with the other values of the population vector (N^{NB}, N^2, N^1) fixed at their 2007 reconstructed values.

Northern Pintails

The Flyway Councils have long identified the northern pintail as a high-priority species for inclusion in the AHM process. In 1997, the USFWS adopted a pintail harvest strategy to help align harvest opportunity with population status, while providing a foundation upon which to develop a formal AHM framework. Since 1997, the harvest strategy has undergone a number of technical improvements and policy revisions. However, the strategy continues to be a set of regulatory prescriptions born out of consensus, rather than an optimal strategy derived from agreed-upon population models, management objectives, regulatory alternatives, and measures of uncertainty.

In 2007, the USFWS and Flyway Councils took a major step towards a truly adaptive approach by incorporating alternative models of population dynamics. Two models are considered: one in which harvest is additive to natural mortality, and another in which harvest losses are compensated for by reductions in natural mortality. In the additive model, winter survival rate is a constant, whereas winter survival is density-dependent in the compensatory model. We here provide a summary of these recent modeling efforts. A detailed progress report is available on-line at http://www.fws.gov/migratorybirds/mgmt/ahm/special-topics.htm.

The predicted $cBPOPt$ in year $t + 1$ ($cBPOP_{t+1}$) for the additive harvest mortality model is calculated as

$$cBPOP_{t+1} = \left\{ cBPOP_t s_s (1 + \gamma_R \hat{R}_t) - \hat{H}_t / (1 - c) \right\} s_w$$

where $cBPOP_t$ is the latitude-adjusted breeding population size in year t, s_s and s_w are the summer and winter survival rates, respectively, γ_R is a bias-correction constant for the age-ratio, c is the crippling loss rate, $\hat{R}_t$ is the predicted age-ratio, and $\hat{H}_t$ is the predicted continental harvest. Discussion of $\hat{R}_t$ and $\hat{H}_t$ submodels are found in the following sections. The model uses the following constants: $s_s = 0.07$, $s_w = 0.93$, $\gamma_R = 0.8$, and $c = 0.20$.

The compensatory harvest mortality model serves as a hypothesis that stands in contrast to the additive harvest mortality model, positing a strong but realistic degree of compensation. The compensatory model assumes that the mechanism for compensation is density-dependent post-harvest (winter) survival. The form is a logistic relationship between winter survival and post-harvest population size, with the relationship anchored around the historic mean values for each variable. For the compensatory model then, predicted winter survival rate in year t (s_t) is calculated as

$$s_t = s_0 + (s_1 - s_0)\left[1 + e^{-(a+b(P_t - \bar{P}))}\right]^{-1},$$

where s_1 (upper asymptote) is 1.0, s_0 (lower asymptote) is 0.7, b (slope term) is -1.0, P_t is the post-harvest population size in year t (expressed in millions), $\bar{P}$ is the mean post-harvest population size (4.295 million from 1974 through 2005), and

$$a = \text{logit}\left(\frac{\bar{s} - s_0}{s_1 - s_0}\right)$$

or

$$a = \log\left(\frac{\bar{s} - s_0}{s_1 - s_0}\right) - \log\left\{1 - \left(\frac{\bar{s} - s_0}{s_1 - s_0}\right)\right\},$$

where $\bar{s}$ is 0.93 (mean winter survival rate).

At moderate population size and latitude, the compensatory model allows for greater harvest (Fig. 10) than does the additive model (note especially that the size of the restrictive region [season-within-a-season] is smaller and is invoked when the latitude is higher). Also, 2- and 3-bird bag limits are called for under more circumstances. But, at high population sizes, the higher bag limits are called for less often, because the compensatory model predicts that growth of the population will be slower (density-dependence).

The fit to historic data was used to compare the additive and compensatory harvest models. From the $cBPOP_t$, $mLAT_t$, and observed harvest (H_t) for the period 1974–through year t, the subsequent year's breeding population size (on the latitude-adjusted scale) was predicted with both the additive and compensatory model, and

25

compared to the observed breeding population size (on the latitude-adjusted scale). The mean-squared error of the predictions from the additive model (MSE_{add}) was calculated as:

$$MSE_{add} = \frac{1}{(t-1975)+1} \sum_{t=1975}^{t} (cBPOP_t - cBPOP_t^{add})^2$$

and the mean-squared error of the predictions from the compensatory model were calculated in a similar manner.

The model weights for the additive and compensatory model were calculated from their relative mean-squared errors. The model weight for the additive model (W_{add}) was calculated as:

$$W_{add} = \frac{\dfrac{1}{MSE_{add}}}{\dfrac{1}{MSE_{add}} + \dfrac{1}{MSE_{comp}}}.$$

The model weight for the compensatory model was found in a corresponding manner, or by subtracting the additive model weight from 1.0. As of 2007, the compensatory model did not fit the historic data as well as the additive model; the model weights were 0.597 for the additive model and 0.403 for the compensatory model, unchanged from 2006. The 2007 average model calls for a strategy that is intermediate between the additive and compensatory models (Fig. 9).

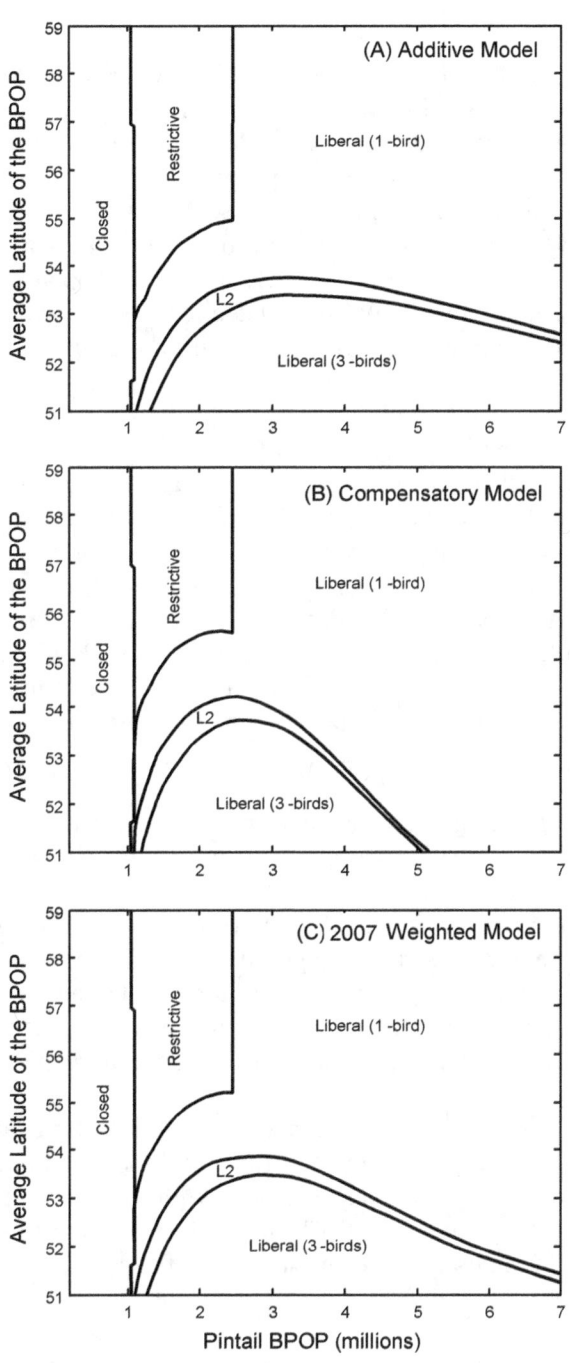

Fig. 9. State-dependent harvest strategy for northern pintails with (A) additive, (B) compensatory, and (C) 2007 weighted models. In each case the strategy assumes that

27

Scaup

In 2007, the USFWS proposed an assessment and decision-making framework to inform scaup harvest management (Boomer and Johnson 2007). This framework was not adopted, partly in response to concerns raised by the waterfowl management community that argued for a delay in implementation to facilitate the discussion of the outstanding technical and policy issues relating to the proposed scaup decision-making framework. In response to this call for increased communication, the USFWS addressed a wide range of questions and concerns regarding the proposed strategy at the 2007 AHM working group meeting. A key outcome of this meeting was the recommendation of the AHM working group for the USFWS to develop an alternative model that would capture the belief that the scaup population will continue to decline to some lower equilibrium level in response to a declining carrying capacity and that harvest at current levels will be completely compensatory. As a result, the USFWS agreed to consider the development of this alternative model.

To further our communication efforts with the Flyways, we outlined methods to facilitate the specification of regulatory alternatives for scaup harvest management (Boomer et al. 2007). We proposed harvest thresholds to be considered under regulatory packages based on a simulation of an optimal policy that was derived under an objective to achieve 95% of the long term cumulative harvest. We used an objective of 95% because it results in a strategy less sensitive to small change in population size as compared to a strategy derived under an objective to achieve 100% of long term cumulative harvest. In addition, the 95% objective allows for some harvest opportunity at relatively low population sizes. We have continued to work with the Flyways to determine what regulations would achieve the allowable harvest thresholds set forth in the scoping document (Boomer et al. 2007). Decisions regarding Flyway specific regulations will be discussed and finalized during this year's late season regulations meetings.

This year, the USFWS Migratory Bird Regulations Committee decided to implement the scaup decision-making framework as proposed in 2007, while also supporting the development of an alternative model.

The lack of scaup demographic information over a sufficient timeframe and at a continental scale precludes the use of a traditional balance equation to represent scaup population and harvest dynamics. As a result, we used a discrete-time, stochastic, logistic-growth population model to represent changes in scaup abundance, while explicitly accounting for scaling issues associated with the monitoring data. Details describing the modeling and assessment framework that has been developed for scaup can be found in Appendix 6.

We updated the scaup assessment based on the current model formulation and data extending from 1974 through 2007. As in past analyses, the state space formulation and Bayesian analysis framework provided reasonable fits to the observed breeding population and total harvest estimates with realistic measures of variation. The posterior mean estimate of the intrinsic rate of increase (r) is 0.101 while the posterior mean estimate of the carrying capacity (K) is 8.38 million birds. The posterior mean estimate of the scaling parameter (q) is 0.537, ranging between 0.464 and 0.620 with 95% probability.

We calculated an optimal regulatory strategy for scaup harvest management based on: (1) a control variable of total harvest (U.S. and Canada combined), (2) current population model and updated parameter estimates, and (3) an objective to achieve 95% of the long-term cumulative harvest. We simulated the use of this regulatory strategy to determine expected performance characteristics. Assuming that harvest management adhered to this strategy

28

(and that current model parameters accurately reflect population dynamics), breeding-population size would be expected to average 4.59 million (SD = 0.87 million). Based on an estimated breeding population size of 3.74 million scaup, the optimal harvest level for scaup is 200 thousand (Table 11). Based on the harvest thresholds specified in the scoping document, this year's optimal harvest would correspond to the restrictive regulatory alternative.

The USFWS intends to continue to work with the Flyways to determine acceptable harvest-management objectives and regulatory alternatives to be used in the decision-making framework for scaup harvest management. Ultimately, we would like to work towards the establishment of scaup regulatory alternatives to be finalized during next year's early season regulations process. Through collaboration with the Flyways, we will continue to develop predicted harvest distributions associated with each Flyway's regulatory alternatives so that these predictions will then form a basis to specify a set of regulatory packages as the control variable to be used in the derivation of next year's optimal regulatory alternative. Moreover, the USFWS will work toward continued collaboration with the waterfowl management community as we move forward with the development of an alternative model to predict scaup population dynamics.

Table 11. Optimal scaup harvest levels (observed scale in millions) and corresponding breeding population sizes (in millions). This strategy is based on the current scaup population model, and an objective to maximize 95% of long-term cumulative harvest. The shaded cell indicates the optimal harvest level for 2008.

BPOP	Optimal Harvest
1.0 – 1.9	0
2.0 – 2.5	0.05
2.6 – 3.0	0.1
3.1 – 3.3	0.15
3.4 – 3.8	0.2
3.9 – 4.1	0.25
4.2 – 4.4	0.3
4.5 – 4.8	0.35
4.9 – 5.1	0.4

LITERATURE CITED

Anderson, D. R., and K. P. Burnham. 1976. Population ecology of the mallard. VI. The effect of exploitation on survival. U.S. Fish and Wildlife Service Resource Publication No. 128. 66pp.

Blohm, R. J. 1989. Introduction to harvest - understanding surveys and season setting. Proceedings of the International Waterfowl Symposium 6:118–133.

Blohm, R. J., R. E. Reynolds, J. P. Bladen, J. D. Nichols, J. E. Hines, K. P. Pollock, and R. T. Eberhardt. 1987. Mallard mortality rates on key breeding and wintering areas. Transactions of the North American Wildlife and Natural Resources Conference 52:246–263.

Boomer, G. S., and F. A. Johnson. 2007. A proposed assessment and decision-making framework to inform scaup harvest management. Unpublished Report. U. S. Fish and Wildlife Service, Laurel, MD. 26pp. [online] URL: http://www.fws.gov/migratorybirds/reports/SpecialTopics/SCAUP2007ReportFINAL.pdf

Boomer, G. S., F. A. Johnson, M. D. Koneff, T. A. Sanders, and R. E. Trost. 2007. A process to determine scaup regulatory alternatives. Unpublished Scoping Document. U. S. Fish and Wildlife Service, Laurel, MD. 20pp. [online] URL:http://www.fws.gov/migratorybirds/reports/SpecialTopics/scaup_regs_scoping_draftVI.pdf

Brooks, S. P., and A. Gelman. 1998 Alternative methods for monitoring convergence of iterative simulations. Journal of Computational and Graphical Statistics 7:434–455.

Burnham, K. P., G. C. White, and D. R. Anderson. 1984. Estimating the effect of hunting on annual survival rates of adult mallards. Journal of Wildlife Management 48:350–361.

Conroy, M. J., M. W. Miller, and J. E. Hines. 2002. Identification and synthetic modeling of factors affecting American black duck populations. Wildlife Monographs 150. 64pp.

Henny, C. J., and Burnham, K. P. 1976. A reward band study of mallards to estimate reporting rates. Journal of Wildlife Management. 40:1–14.

Heusman, H W, and J. R. Sauer. 2000. The northeastern states' waterfowl breeding population survey. Wildlife Society Bulletin 28:355–364.

Hodges, J. L., J. G. King, B. Conant, and H. A. Hanson. 1996. Aerial surveys of waterbirds in Alaska 1975–94: population trends and observer variability. Information and Technology Report 4, National Biological Service, U.S. Dept. of the Interior, Washington, D.C. 25pp.

Johnson, F. A. 2003. Population dynamics of ducks other than mallards in mid-continent North America. Draft. Fish and Wildlife Service, U.S. Dept. Interior, Washington, D.C. 15pp.

Johnson, F. A., J. A. Dubovsky, M. C. Runge, and D. R. Eggeman. 2002a. A revised protocol for the adaptive harvest management of eastern mallards. Fish and Wildlife Service, U.S. Dept. Interior, Washington, D.C. 13pp. [online] URL: http://migratorybirds.fws.gov/reports/ahm02/emal-ahm-2002.pdf.

Johnson, F. A., W. L. Kendall, and J. A. Dubovsky. 2002b. Conditions and limitations on learning in the adaptive management of mallard harvests. Wildlife Society Bulletin 30:176–185.

Johnson, F. A., C. T. Moore, W. L. Kendall, J. A. Dubovsky, D. F. Caithamer, J. R. Kelley, Jr., and B. K. Williams. 1997. Uncertainty and the management of mallard harvests. Journal of Wildlife Management 61:202–216.

Johnson, F. A., and B. K. Williams. 1999. Protocol and practice in the adaptive management of waterfowl harvests. Conservation Ecology 3(1): 8. [online] URL: http://www.consecol.org/vol3/iss1/art8.

Johnson, F. A., B. K. Williams, J. D. Nichols, J. E. Hines, W. L. Kendall, G. W. Smith, and D. F. Caithamer. 1993. Developing an adaptive management strategy for harvesting waterfowl in North America. Transactions of the North American Wildlife and Natural Resources Conference 58:565–583.

Johnson, F. A., B. K. Williams, and P. R. Schmidt. 1996. Adaptive decision-making in waterfowl harvest and habitat management. Proceedings of the International Waterfowl Symposium 7:26–33.

Link, W. A., J. R. Sauer, and D. K. Niven. 2006. A hierarchical model for regional analysis of population change using Christmas bird count data, with application to the American black duck. The Condor 108:13–24.

Lubow, B. C. 1995. SDP: Generalized software for solving stochastic dynamic optimization problems. Wildlife Society Bulletin 23:738–742.

Meyer, R., and R. B. Millar. 1999. BUGS in Bayesian stock assessments. Canadian Journal of Fisheries and Aquatic Sciences 56:1078–1086.

Millar, R. B., and R. Meyer. 2000. Non-linear state space modeling of fisheries biomass dynamics by using Metropolis-Hastings within Gibbs sampling. Applied Statistics 49: 327–342.

Nichols, J. D., F. A. Johnson, and B. K. Williams. 1995a. Managing North American waterfowl in the face of uncertainty. Annual Review of Ecology and Systematics 26:177–199.

Nichols, J. D., Reynolds, R. E., Blohm, R. J. Trost, R. E., Hines, J. E. and Bladen, J. P. 1995b. Geographic variation in band reporting rates for mallards based on reward banding. Journal of Wildlife Management 59:697–708.

Runge, M. C., F. A. Johnson, J. A. Dubovsky, W. L. Kendall, J. Lawrence, and J. Gammonley. 2002. A revised protocol for the adaptive harvest management of mid-continent mallards. Fish and Wildlife Service, U.S. Dept. Interior, Washington, D.C. 28pp. [online] URL: http://migratorybirds.fws.gov/reports/ahm02/MCMrevise2002.pdf.

Schaefer, M. B. 1954. Some aspects of the dynamics of populations important to the management of commercial marine fisheries. Bulletin of the Inter-American Tropical Tuna Commission 1:25–56.

Smith, G. W. 1995. A critical review of the aerial and ground surveys of breeding waterfowl in North America. Biological Science Report 5, National Biological Service, U.S. Dept. of the Interior, Washington, D.C. 252pp.

Spiegelhalter, D. J., A. Thomas, N. Best, and D. Lunn. 2003. WinBUGS 1.4 User manual. MRC Biostatistics Unit, Institute of Public Health, Cambridge, UK.

U.S. Fish and Wildlife Service. 2000. Adaptive harvest management: 2000 duck hunting season. U.S. Dept. Interior, Washington. D.C. 43pp. [online] URL: http://migratorybirds.fws.gov/reports/ahm00/ahm2000.pdf.

U.S. Fish and Wildlife Service. 2001. Framework-date extensions for duck hunting in the United States: projected impacts & coping with uncertainty, U.S. Dept. Interior, Washington, D.C. 8pp. [online] URL: http://migratorybirds.fws.gov/reports/ahm01/fwassess.pdf.

U.S. Fish and Wildlife Service. 2002. Adaptive harvest management: 2002 duck hunting season. U.S. Dept. Interior, Washington. D.C. 34pp. [online] URL: http://migratorybirds.fws.gov/reports/ahm02/2002-AHM-report.pdf.

Walters, C. J. 1986. Adaptive management of renewable resources. MacMillan Publ. Co., New York, N.Y. 374pp.

Williams, B. K., and F. A. Johnson. 1995. Adaptive management and the regulation of waterfowl harvests. Wildlife Society Bulletin 23:430–436.

Williams, B. K., F. A. Johnson, and K. Wilkins. 1996. Uncertainty and the adaptive management of waterfowl harvests. Journal of Wildlife Management 60:223–232.

APPENDIX 1: AHM Working Group

(Note: This list includes only permanent members of the AHM Working Group. Not listed here are numerous persons from federal and state agencies that assist the Working Group on an ad-hoc basis.)

Coordinator:

Mark Koneff
U.S. Fish & Wildlife Service
11510 American Holly Drive
Laurel, Maryland 20708-4017
phone: 301-497-5648
fax: 301-497-5871
e-mail: mark_koneff@fws.gov

USFWS Representatives:

Bob Blohm (Region 9)
U.S. Fish and Wildlife Service
4401 N Fairfax Drive
MS MSP-4107
Arlington, VA 22203
phone: 703-358-1966
fax: 703-358-2272
e-mail: robert_blohm@fws.gov

Brad Bortner (Region 1)
U.S. Fish and Wildlife Service
911 NE 11th Ave.
Portland, OR 97232-4181
phone: 503-231-6164
fax: 503-231-2364
e-mail: brad_bortner@fws.gov

Dave Case (contractor)
D.J. Case & Associates
607 Lincolnway West
Mishawaka, IN 46544
phone: 574-258-0100
fax: 574-258-0189
e-mail: dave@djcase.com

Jim Dubovsky (Region 6)
U.S. Fish and Wildlife Service
P.O. Box 25486-DFC
Denver, CO 80225-0486
phone: 303-236-4403
fax: 303-236-8680
e-mail:james_dubovsky@fws.gov

Diane Pence (Region 5)

Jeff Haskins (Region 2)
U.S. Fish and Wildlife Service
P.O. Box 1306
Albuquerque, NM 87103
phone: 505-248-6827 (ext 30)
fax: 505-248-7885
e-mail: jeff_haskins@fws.gov

Jim Kelley (Region 9)
U.S. Fish and Wildlife Service
1 Federal Drive
Fort Snelling, MN 55111-0458
phone: 612-713-5409
fax: 612-713-5393
e-mail: james_r_kelley@fws.gov

Sean Kelly (Region 3)
U.S. Fish and Wildlife Service
1 Federal Drive
Ft. Snelling, MN 55111-4056
phone: 612-713-5470
fax: 612-713-5393
e-mail: sean_kelly@fws.gov

Paul Padding (Region 9)
U.S. Fish and Wildlife Service
11510 American Holly Drive
Laurel, MD 20708
phone: 301-497-5851
fax: 301-497-5885
e-mail: paul_padding@fws.gov

Bob Trost (Region 9)

U.S. Fish and Wildlife Service
300 Westgate Center Drive
Hadley, MA 01035-9589
phone: 413-253-8577
fax: 413-253-8424
e-mail: diane_pence@fws.gov

Russ Oates (Region 7)
U.S. Fish and Wildlife Service
1011 East Tudor Road
Anchorage, AK 99503-6119
phone: 907-786-3446
fax: 907-786-3641
e-mail: russ_oates@fws.gov

Dave Sharp (Region 9)
U.S. Fish and Wildlife Service
P.O. Box 25486, DFC
Denver, CO 80225-0486
phone: 303-275-2386
fax: 303-275-2384
e-mail: dave_sharp@fws.gov

U.S. Fish and Wildlife Service
911 NE 11th Ave.
Portland, OR 97232-4181
phone: 503-231-6162
fax: 503-231-6228
e-mail: robert_trost@fws.gov

David Viker (Region 4)
U.S. Fish and Wildlife Service
1875 Century Blvd., Suite 345
Atlanta, GA 30345
phone: 404-679-7188
fax: 404-679-7285
e-mail: david_viker@fws.gov

Canadian Wildlife Service Representatives:

Dale Caswell
Canadian Wildlife Service
123 Main St. Suite 150
Winnipeg, Manitoba, Canada R3C 4W2
phone: 204-983-5260
fax: 204-983-5248
e-mail: dale.caswell@ec.gc.ca

Eric Reed
Canadian Wildlife Service
351 St. Joseph Boulevard
Hull, QC K1A OH3, Canada
phone: 819-953-0294
fax: 819-953-6283
e-mail: eric.reed@ec.gc.ca

Flyway Council Representatives:

Min Huang (Atlantic Flyway)
CT Dept. of Environmental Protection
Franklin Wildlife Mgmt. Area
391 Route 32
North Franklin, CT 06254, USA
Phone: 860/642-6528
fax: 860/642-7964
e-mail: min.huang@po.state.ct.us

Mike Johnson (Central Flyway)
North Dakota Game and Fish Department
100 North Bismarck Expressway
Bismarck, ND 58501-5095
phone: 701-328-6319
fax: 701-328-6352
e-mail: mjohnson@state.nd.us

Bryan Swift (Atlantic Flyway)
Dept. Environmental Conservation

Larry Reynolds (Mississippi Flyway)
LA Dept. of Wildlife & Fisheries
PO Box 98000
Baton Rouge, LA 70898-9000, USA
Phone: 225/765-0456
Fax: 225/763-5456
e-mail: lreynolds@wlf.state.la.us

Jon Runge (Pacific Flyway)
Colorado Division of Wildlife
317 W. Prospect
Fort Collins, CO 80526
Phone: 970-472-4365
e-mail: Jon.Runge@state.co.us

Dan Yparraguirre (Pacific Flyway)
California Dept. of Fish and Game

625 Broadway
Albany, NY 12233-4754
phone: 518-402-8866
fax: 518-402-9027 or 402-8925
e-mail: blswift@gw.dec.state.ny.us

Mark Vrtiska (Central Flyway)
Nebraska Game and Parks Commission
P.O. Box 30370
2200 North 33rd Street
Lincoln, NE 68503-1417
phone: 402-471-5437
fax: 402-471-5528
email: mvrtiska@ngpc.state.ne.us

1812 Ninth Street
Sacramento, CA 95814
phone: 916-445-3685
e-mail: dyparraguirre@dfg.ca.gov

Guy Zenner (Mississippi Flyway)
Iowa Dept. of Natural Resources
1203 North Shore Drive
Clear Lake, IA   50428
phone: 515-357-3517, ext. 23
fax: 515-357-5523
e-mail: gzenner@netins.net

APPENDIX 2: Mid-continent Mallard Models

In 1995, we developed population models to predict changes in midcontinent mallards based on the traditional survey area which includes individuals from Alaska (Johnson et al. 1997). In 1997, we added mallards from the Great Lakes region (Michigan, Minnesota, and Wisconsin) to the mid-continent mallard stock, assuming their population dynamics were equivalent. In 2002, we made extensive revisions to the set of alternative models describing the population dynamics of mid-continent mallards (Runge et al. 2002, USFWS 2002). This year we have redefined the population of mid-continent mallards to account for the removal of Alaskan birds (WBPHS strata 1–12) that are now considered to be in the western mallard stock and have subsequently rescaled the model set appropriately.

Model Structure

Collectively, the models express uncertainty (or disagreement) about whether harvest is an additive or compensatory form of mortality (Burnham et al. 1984), and whether the reproductive process is weakly or strongly density-dependent (i.e., the degree to which reproductive rates decline with increasing population size).

All population models for mid-continent mallards share a common "balance equation" to predict changes in breeding-population size as a function of annual survival and reproductive rates:

$$N_{t+1} = N_t \left(m S_{t,AM} + (1-m)\left(S_{t,AF} + R_t \left(S_{t,JF} + S_{t,JM}\, \phi_F^{sum} / \phi_M^{sum} \right) \right) \right)$$

where:
N = breeding population size,
m = proportion of males in the breeding population,
S_{AM}, S_{AF}, S_{JF}, and S_{JM} = survival rates of adult males, adult females, young females, and young males, respectively,
R = reproductive rate, defined as the fall age ratio of females,
$\phi_F^{sum} / \phi_M^{sum}$ = the ratio of female (F) to male (M) summer survival, and
t = year.

We assumed that m and $\phi_F^{sum} / \phi_M^{sum}$ are fixed and known. We also assumed, based in part on information provided by Blohm et al. (1987), the ratio of female to male summer survival was equivalent to the ratio of annual survival rates in the absence of harvest. Based on this assumption, we estimated $\phi_F^{sum} / \phi_M^{sum} = 0.897$. To estimate m we expressed the balance equation in matrix form:

$$\begin{bmatrix} N_{t+1,AM} \\ N_{t+1,AF} \end{bmatrix} = \begin{bmatrix} S_{AM} & RS_{JM}\, \phi_F^{sum} / \phi_M^{sum} \\ 0 & S_{AF} + RS_{JF} \end{bmatrix} \begin{bmatrix} N_{t,AM} \\ N_{t,AF} \end{bmatrix}$$

and substituted the constant ratio of summer survival and means of estimated survival and reproductive rates. The right eigenvector of the transition matrix is the stable sex structure that the breeding population eventually would attain with these constant demographic rates. This eigenvector yielded an estimate of $m = 0.5246$.

Using estimates of annual survival and reproductive rates, the balance equation for mid-continent mallards over-predicted observed population sizes by 11.0% on average. The source of the bias is unknown, so we modified the balance equation to eliminate the bias by adjusting both survival and reproductive rates:

$$N_{t+1} = \gamma_S N_t \left(m S_{t,AM} + (1-m)\left(S_{t,AF} + \gamma_R R_t \left(S_{t,JF} + S_{t,JM} \, \phi_F^{sum} / \phi_M^{sum} \right) \right) \right)$$

where γ denotes the bias-correction factors for survival (S) and reproduction (R). We used a least squares approach to estimate $\gamma_S = 0.9407$ and $\gamma_R = 0.8647$.

Survival Process

We considered two alternative hypotheses for the relationship between annual survival and harvest rates. For both models, we assumed that survival in the absence of harvest was the same for adults and young of the same sex. In the model where harvest mortality is additive to natural mortality:

$$S_{t,sex,age} = s_{0,sex}^A \left(1 - K_{t,sex,age} \right)$$

and in the model where changes in natural mortality compensate for harvest losses (up to some threshold):

$$S_{t,sex,age} = \begin{cases} s_{0,sex}^C & \text{if } K_{t,sex,age} \le 1 - s_{0,sex}^C \\ 1 - K_{t,sex,age} & \text{if } K_{t,sex,age} > 1 - s_{0,sex}^C \end{cases}$$

where s_0 = survival in the absence of harvest under the additive (A) or compensatory (C) model, and K = harvest rate adjusted for crippling loss (20%, Anderson and Burnham 1976). We averaged estimates of s_0 across banding reference areas by weighting by breeding-population size. For the additive model, $s_0 = 0.7896$ and 0.6886 for males and females, respectively. For the compensatory model, $s_0 = 0.6467$ and 0.5965 for males and females, respectively. These estimates may seem counterintuitive because survival in the absence of harvest should be the same for both models. However, estimating a common (but still sex-specific) s_0 for both models leads to alternative models that do not fit available band-recovery data equally well. More importantly, it suggests that the greatest uncertainty about survival rates is when harvest rate is within the realm of experience. By allowing s_0 to differ between additive and compensatory models, we acknowledge that the greatest uncertainty about survival rate is its value in the absence of harvest (i.e., where we have no experience).

Reproductive Process

Annual reproductive rates were estimated from age ratios in the harvest of females, corrected using a constant estimate of differential vulnerability. Predictor variables were the number of ponds in May in Prairie Canada (P, in millions) and the size of the breeding population (N, in millions). We estimated the best-fitting linear model, and then calculated the 80% confidence ellipsoid for all model parameters. We chose the two points on this ellipsoid with the largest and smallest values for the effect of breeding-population size, and generated a weakly density-dependent model:

$$R_t = 0.7166 + 0.1083 P_t - 0.0373 N_t$$

and a strongly density-dependent model:

$$R_t = 1.1390 + 0.1376 P_t - 0.1131 N_t$$

Predicted recruitment was then rescaled to reflect the current definition of mid-continent mallards which now excludes birds from Alaska but includes mallards observed in the Great Lakes region.

Pond Dynamics

We modeled annual variation in Canadian pond numbers as a first-order autoregressive process. The estimated model was:

$$P_{t+1} = 2.2127 + 0.3420 P_t + \varepsilon_t$$

where ponds are in millions and ε_t is normally distributed with mean = 0 and variance = 1.2567.

Variance of Prediction Errors

Using the balance equation and sub-models described above, predictions of breeding-population size in year $t+1$ depend only on specification of population size, pond numbers, and harvest rate in year t. For the period in which comparisons were possible, we compared these predictions with observed population sizes.

We estimated the prediction-error variance by setting:

$$e_t = \ln\left(N_t^{obs}\right) - \ln\left(N_t^{pre}\right)$$

then assuming $e_t \sim N\left(0, \sigma^2\right)$

and estimating $\hat{\sigma}^2 = \sum_t \left[\ln\left(N_t^{obs}\right) - \ln\left(N_t^{pre}\right)\right]^2 \Big/ (n-1)$

where *obs* and *pre* are observed and predicted population sizes (in millions), respectively, and n = the number of years being compared. We were concerned about a variance estimate that was too small, either by chance or because the number of years in which comparisons were possible was small. Therefore, we calculated the upper 80% confidence limit for σ^2 based on a Chi-squared distribution for each combination of the alternative survival and reproductive sub-models, and then averaged them. The final estimate of σ^2 was 0.0280, equivalent to a coefficient of variation of about 18%.

Model Implications

The population model with additive hunting mortality and weakly density-dependent recruitment (SaRw) leads to the most conservative harvest strategy, whereas the model with compensatory hunting mortality and strongly density-dependent recruitment (ScRs) leads to the most liberal strategy. The other two models (SaRs and ScRw) lead to strategies that are intermediate between these extremes. Under the models with compensatory hunting mortality (ScRs and ScRw), the optimal strategy is to have a liberal regulation regardless of population size or number of ponds because at harvest rates achieved under the liberal alternative, harvest has no effect on population size. Under the strongly density-dependent model (ScRs), the density-dependence regulates the population and keeps it within narrow bounds. Under the weakly density-dependent model (ScRw), the density-dependence does not exert as strong a regulatory effect, and the population size fluctuates more.

Model Weights

Model weights are calculated as Bayesian probabilities, reflecting the relative ability of the individual alternative models to predict observed changes in population size. The Bayesian probability for each model is a function of the model's previous (or prior) weight and the likelihood of the observed population size under that model. We used Bayes' theorem to calculate model weights from a comparison of predicted and observed population sizes for the years 1996–2008, starting with equal model weights in 1995.

APPENDIX 3: Eastern Mallard Models

Model Structure

We also revised the population models for eastern mallards in 2002 (Johnson et al. 2002a, USFWS 2002). The current set of six models: (1) relies solely on federal and state waterfowl surveys (rather than the Breeding Bird Survey) to estimate abundance; (2) allows for the possibility of a positive bias in estimates of survival or reproductive rates; (3) incorporates competing hypotheses of strongly and weakly density-dependent reproduction; and (4) assumes that hunting mortality is additive to other sources of mortality.

As with mid-continent mallards, all population models for eastern mallards share a common balance equation to predict changes in breeding-population size as a function of annual survival and reproductive rates:

$$N_{t+1} = N_t \cdot \left(\left(p \cdot S_t^{am} \right) + \left((1-p) \cdot S_t^{af} \right) + \left(p \cdot \left(A_t^m / d \right) \cdot S_t^{ym} \right) + \left(p \cdot \left(A_t^m / d \right) \cdot \psi \cdot S_t^{yf} \right) \right)$$

where:
N = breeding-population size,
p = proportion of males in the breeding population,
S^{am}, S^{af}, S^{ym}, and S^{yf} = survival rates of adult males, adult females, young males, and young females, respectively,
A^m = ratio of young males to adult males in the harvest,
d = ratio of young male to adult male direct recovery rates,
ψ = the ratio of male to female summer survival, and t = year.

In this balance equation, we assume that p, d, and ψ are fixed and known. The parameter ψ is necessary to account for the difference in anniversary date between the breeding-population survey (May) and the survival and reproductive rate estimates (August). This model also assumes that the sex ratio of fledged young is 1:1; hence A^m/d appears twice in the balance equation. We estimated $d = 1.043$ as the median ratio of young:adult male band-recovery rates in those states from which wing receipts were obtained. We estimated $\psi = 1.216$ by regressing through the origin estimates of male survival against female survival in the absence of harvest, assuming that differences in natural mortality between males and females occur principally in summer. To estimate p, we used a population projection matrix of the form:

$$\begin{bmatrix} M_{t+1} \\ F_{t+1} \end{bmatrix} = \begin{bmatrix} S^{am} + \left(A^m / d \right) \cdot S^{ym} & 0 \\ \left(A^m / d \right) \cdot \psi \cdot S^{yf} & S^{af} \end{bmatrix} \cdot \begin{bmatrix} M_t \\ F_t \end{bmatrix}$$

where M and F are the relative number of males and females in the breeding populations, respectively. To parameterize the projection matrix we used average annual survival rate and age ratio estimates, and the estimates of d and ψ provided above. The right eigenvector of the projection matrix is the stable proportion of males and females the breeding population eventually would attain in the face of constant demographic rates. This eigenvector yielded an estimate of $p = 0.544$.

We also attempted to determine whether estimates of survival and reproductive rates were unbiased. We relied on the balance equation provided above, except that we included additional parameters to correct for any bias that might exist. Because we were unsure of the source(s) of potential bias, we alternatively assumed that any bias resided solely in survival rates:

$$N_{t+1} = N_t \cdot \Omega \cdot \left(\left(p \cdot S_t^{am} \right) + \left((1-p) \cdot S_t^{af} \right) + \left(p \cdot \left(A_t^m / d \right) \cdot S_t^{ym} \right) + \left(p \cdot \left(A_t^m / d \right) \cdot \psi \cdot S_t^{yf} \right) \right)$$

(where Ω is the bias-correction factor for survival rates), or solely in reproductive rates:

$$N_{t+1} = N_t \cdot \left(\left(p \cdot S_t^{am} \right) + \left((1-p) \cdot S_t^{af} \right) + \left(p \cdot \alpha \cdot \left(A_t^m / d \right) \cdot S_t^{ym} \right) + \left(p \cdot \alpha \cdot \left(A_t^m / d \right) \cdot \psi \cdot S_t^{yf} \right) \right)$$

(where α is the bias-correction factor for reproductive rates). We estimated Ω and α by determining the values of these parameters that minimized the sum of squared differences between observed and predicted population sizes. Based on this analysis, $\Omega = 0.836$ and $\alpha = 0.701$, suggesting a positive bias in survival or reproductive rates. However, because of the limited number of years available for comparing observed and predicted population sizes, we also retained the balance equation that assumes estimates of survival and reproductive rates are unbiased.

Survival Process

For purposes of AHM, annual survival rates must be predicted based on the specification of regulation-specific harvest rates (and perhaps on other uncontrolled factors). Annual survival for each age (i) and sex (j) class under a given regulatory alternative is:

$$S_t^{i,j} = \overline{\theta}^j \cdot \left(1 - \frac{\left(h_t^{am} \cdot v^{i,j} \right)}{(1-c)} \right)$$

where:

S = annual survival,

$\overline{\theta}^j$ = mean survival from natural causes,

h^{am} = harvest rate of adult males, and

v = harvest vulnerability relative to adult males,

c = rate of crippling (unretrieved harvest).

This model assumes that annual variation in survival is due solely to variation in harvest rates, that relative harvest vulnerability of the different age-sex classes is fixed and known, and that survival from natural causes is fixed at its sample mean. We estimated $\overline{\theta}^j = 0.7307$ and 0.5950 for males and females, respectively.

Reproductive process

As with survival, annual reproductive rates must be predicted in advance of setting regulations. We relied on the apparent relationship between breeding-population size and reproductive rates:

$$R_t = a \cdot \exp(b \cdot N_t)$$

where R_t is the reproductive rate (i.e., A_t^m / d), N_t is breeding-population size in millions, and a and b are model parameters. The least-squares parameter estimates were $a = 2.508$ and $b = -0.875$. Because of both the importance and uncertainty of the relationship between population size and reproduction, we specified two alternative models in which the slope (b) was fixed at the least-squares estimate $\pm$ one standard error, and in which the intercepts (a) were subsequently re-estimated. This provided alternative hypotheses of strongly density-dependent ($a = 4.154$, $b = -1.377$) and weakly density-dependent reproduction ($a = 1.518$, $b = -0.373$).

Variance of Prediction Errors

Using the balance equations and sub-models provided above, predictions of breeding-population size in year $t+1$ depend only on the specification of a regulatory alternative and on an estimate of population size in year t. For the period in which comparisons were possible (1991–96), we were interested in how well these predictions corresponded with observed population sizes. In making these comparisons, we were primarily concerned with how well the bias-corrected balance equations and reproductive and survival sub-models performed. Therefore, we relied on estimates of harvest rates rather than regulations as model inputs.

We estimated the prediction-error variance by setting:

$$e_t = \ln\left(N_t^{obs}\right) - \ln\left(N_t^{pre}\right)$$

$$\text{then assuming} \quad e_t \sim N\left(0, \sigma^2\right)$$

$$\text{and estimating} \quad \hat{\sigma}^2 = \sum_t \left[\ln\left(N_t^{obs}\right) - \ln\left(N_t^{pre}\right)\right]^2 \bigg/ n$$

where *obs* and *pre* are observed and predicted population sizes (in millions), respectively, and $n = 6$.

Variance estimates were similar regardless of whether we assumed that the bias was in reproductive rates or in survival, or whether we assumed that reproduction was strongly or weakly density-dependent. Thus, we averaged variance estimates to provide a final estimate of $\sigma^2 = 0.006$, which is equivalent to a coefficient of variation (*CV*) of 8.0%. We were concerned, however, about the small number of years available for estimating this variance. Therefore, we estimated an 80% confidence interval for σ^2 based on a Chi-squared distribution and used the upper limit for $\sigma^2 = 0.018$ (i.e., $CV = 14.5\%$) to express the additional uncertainty about the magnitude of prediction errors attributable to potentially important environmental effects not expressed by the models.

Model Implications

Model-specific regulatory strategies based on the hypothesis of weakly density-dependent reproduction are considerably more conservative than those based on the hypothesis of strongly density-dependent reproduction. The three models with weakly density-dependent reproduction suggest a carrying capacity (i.e., average population size in the absence of harvest) >2.0 million mallards, and prescribe extremely restrictive regulations for population size <1.0 million. The three models with strongly density-dependent reproduction suggest a carrying capacity of about 1.5 million mallards, and prescribe liberal regulations for population sizes >300 thousand. Optimal regulatory strategies are relatively insensitive to whether models include a bias correction or not. All model-specific regulatory strategies are "knife-edged," meaning that large differences in the optimal regulatory choice can be precipitated by only small changes in breeding-population size. This result is at least partially due to the small differences in predicted harvest rates among the current regulatory alternatives (see the section on Regulatory Alternatives later in this report).

Model Weights

We used Bayes' theorem to calculate model weights from a comparison of predicted and observed population sizes for the years 1996–2008. We calculated weights for the alternative models based on an assumption of equal model weights in 1996 (the last year data was used to develop most model components) and on estimates of year-specific harvest rates (Appendix 5).

41

APPENDIX 4: Western Mallard Models

In contrast to mid-continent and eastern mallards, we did not model changes in population size of western mallards as an explicit function of survival and reproductive rate estimates (which in turn may be functions of harvest and environmental covariates). We believed this so-called "balance-equation approach" was not viable for western mallards because of insufficient banding in Alaska to estimate survival rates, and because of the difficulty in estimating stock-specific fall age ratios from a sample of wings derived from a mix of breeding stocks. We therefore relied on a discrete logistic model (Schaefer 1954), which combines reproduction and natural mortality into a single parameter r, the intrinsic rate of growth. The model assumes density-dependent growth, which is regulated by the ratio of population size, N, to the carrying capacity of the environment, K (i.e., equilibrium population size in the absence of harvest). In the traditional formulation, harvest mortality is additive to other sources of mortality, but compensation for hunting losses can occur through subsequent increases in production. However, we parameterized the model in a way that also allows for compensation of harvest mortality between the hunting and breeding seasons. It is important to note that compensation modeled in this way is purely phenomenological, in the sense that there is no explicit ecological mechanism for compensation (e.g., density-dependent mortality after the hunting season).

The basic model for both the Alaska and California/Oregon stocks had the form:

$$N_{t+1} = \left[N_t + N_t r \left(1 - \frac{N_t}{K} \right) \right] (1 - \alpha_t)$$

$$where \quad \alpha_t = d \cdot h_t^{AM}$$

and where t = year, h^{AM} = the harvest rate of adult males, and d = a scaling factor. The scaling factor is used to account for a combination of unobservable effects, including un-retrieved harvest (i.e., crippling loss), differential harvest mortality of cohorts other than adult males, and for the possibility that some harvest mortality may not affect subsequent breeding-population size (i.e., the compensatory mortality hypothesis).

Estimation Framework

We used Bayesian estimation methods in combination with a state-space model that accounts explicitly for both process and observation error in breeding population size. This combination of methods is becoming widely used in natural resource modeling, in part because it facilitates the fitting of non-linear models that may have non-normal errors (Meyer and Millar 1999). The Bayesian approach also provides a natural and intuitive way to portray uncertainty, allows one to incorporate prior information about model parameters, and permits the updating of parameter estimates as further information becomes available.

We first scaled N by K as recommended by Meyer and Millar (1999), and assumed that process errors e_t were log-normally distributed with mean 0 and variance σ^2. Thus, the process model had the form:

$$P_t = N_t / K_t$$

$$\log(P_t) = \log\left\{ \left[P_{t-1} + P_{t-1} r (1 - P_{t-1}) \right] \left(1 - d \cdot h_{t-1}^{AM} \right) \right\} + e_t$$

$$where \quad e_t \sim N(0, \sigma^2)$$

The observation model related the unknown population sizes ($P_t K$) to the population sizes (N_t) estimated from the breeding-population surveys in Alaska and California-Oregon. We assumed that the observation process yielded additive, normally distributed errors, which were represented by:

$$N_t = P_t K + \varepsilon_t^{BPOP},$$

$$\text{where} \quad \varepsilon_t^{BPOP} \sim N(0, \sigma_{BPOP}^2).$$

Use of the observation model allowed us to account for the sampling error in population estimates, while permitting us to estimate the process error, which reflects the inability of the model to completely describe changes in population size. The process error reflects the combined effect of misspecification of an appropriate model form, as well as any un-modeled environmental drivers. We initially examined a number of possible environmental covariates, including the Palmer Drought Index in California and Oregon, spring temperature in Alaska, and the El Niño Southern Oscillation Index (http://www.cdc.noaa.gov/people/klaus.wolter/MEI/mei.html). While the estimated effects of these covariates on r or K were generally what one would expect, they were never of sufficient magnitude to have a meaningful effect on optimal harvest strategies. We therefore chose not to further pursue an investigation of environmental covariates, and posited that the process error was a sufficient surrogate for these un-modeled effects.

Parameterization of the models also required measures of harvest rate. Beginning in 2002, harvest rates of adult males were estimated directly from the recovery of reward bands. Prior to 1993, we used direct recoveries of standard bands, corrected for band-reporting rates provided by Nichols et al. (1995b). We also used the band-reporting rates provided by Nichols et al. (1995b) for estimating harvest rates in 1994 and 1995, except that we inflated the reporting rates of full-address and toll-free bands based on an unpublished analysis by Clint Moore and Jim Nichols (Patuxent Wildlife Research Center). We were unwilling to estimate harvest rates for the years 1996–2001 because of suspected, but unknown, increases in the reporting rates of all bands. For simplicity, harvest rate estimates were treated as known values in our analysis, although future analyses might benefit from an appropriate observation model for these data.

In a Bayesian analysis, one is interested in making probabilistic statements about the model parameters (θ), conditioned on the observed data. Thus, we are interested in evaluating P(θ|data), which requires the specification of prior distributions for all model parameters and unobserved system states (θ) and the sampling distribution (likelihood) of the observed data P(data| θ). Using Bayes theorem, we can represent the posterior probability distribution of model parameters, conditioned on the data, as:

$$P(\theta \mid data) \propto P(\theta) \times P(data \mid \theta).$$

Accordingly, we specified prior distributions for model parameters r, K, d, and P_0, which is the initial population size relative to carrying capacity. For both stocks, we specified the following prior distributions for r, d, and σ^2:

$$r \sim Log-normal(-1.0397, 1.4427)$$

$$d \sim Uniform(0, 2)$$

$$\sigma^2 \sim Inverse-gamma(0.001, 0.001)$$

The prior distribution for r is centered at 0.35, which we believe to be a reasonable value for mallards based on life-history characteristics and estimates for other avian species. Yet the distribution also admits considerable uncertainty as to the value of r within what we believe to be realistic biological bounds. As for the harvest-rate scalar, we would expect $d \geq 1$ under the additive hypothesis and $d < 1$ under the compensatory hypothesis. As we had no data to specify an informative prior distribution, we specified a vague prior in which d could take on a wide range of values with equal probability. We used a traditional, uninformative prior distribution for σ^2. Prior distributions for K and P_0 were stock-specific and are described in the following sections.

We used the public-domain software WinBUGS (http://www.mrc-bsu.cam.ac.uk/bugs/) to derive samples from the joint posterior distribution of model parameters via Markov-Chain Monte Carlo (MCMC) simulations. We obtained 510,000 samples from the joint posterior distribution, discarded the first 10,000, and then thinned the remainder by 50, resulting in a final sample of 10,000.

Alaska mallards

Data selection.--Breeding population estimates of mallards in Alaska (and the Old Crow Flats in Yukon) are available since 1955 in WBPHS strata 1–12 (Smith 1995). However, a change in survey aircraft in 1977 instantaneously increased the detectability of waterfowl, and thus population estimates (Hodges et al. 1996). Moreover, there was a rapid increase in average annual temperature in Alaska at the same time, apparently tied to changes in the frequency and intensity of El Niño events (http://www.cdc.noaa.gov/people/klaus.wolter/MEI/mei.html). This confounding of changes in climate and survey methods led us to truncate the years 1955–1977 from the time series of population estimates.

Modeling of the Alaska stock also depended on the availability of harvest-rate estimates derived from band-recovery data. Unfortunately, sufficient numbers of mallards were not banded in Alaska prior to 1990. A search for covariates that would have allowed us to make harvest-rate predictions for years in which band-recovery data were not available was not fruitful, and we were thus forced to further restrict the time-series to 1990–2005. Even so, harvest rate estimates were not available for the years 1996–2001 because of unknown changes in band-reporting rates. Because available estimates of harvest rate showed no apparent variation over time, we simply used the mean and standard deviation of the available estimates and generated independent samples of predictions for the missing years based on a logit transformation and an assumption of normality:

$$\ln\left(\frac{h_t}{1-h_t}\right) \sim Normal(-2.3265, 0.0830) \quad for\ t = 1996 - 2001$$

Prior distributions for K and P_0.—We believed that sufficient information was available to use mildly informative priors for K and P_0. In recent years the Alaska stock has contained approximately 0.8 million mallards. If harvest rates have been comparable to that necessary to achieve maximum sustained yield (MSY) under the logistic model (i.e., $r/2$), then we would expect $K \approx 1.6$ million. On the other hand, if harvest rates have been less than those associated with MSY, then we would expect $K < 1.6$ million. Because we believed it was not likely that harvest rates were $>r/2$, we believed the likely range of K to be 0.8–1.6 million. We therefore specified a prior distribution that had a mean of 1.4 million, but had a sufficiently large variance to admit a wide range of possible values:

$$K \sim Log-normal(0.13035, 0.41224)$$

Extending this line of reasoning, we specified a prior distribution that assumed the estimated population size of approximately 0.4 million at the start of the time-series (i.e., 1990) was 20–60% of K. Thus on a log scale:

$$P_o \sim Uniform(-1.6094, -0.5108)$$

Parameter estimates.—The logistic model and associated posterior parameter estimates provided a reasonable fit to the observed time-series of population estimates. The posterior means of K and r were similar to their priors, although their variances were considerably smaller (albeit still large) (Table a). However, the posterior distribution of d was essentially the same as its prior, reflecting the absence of information in the data necessary to reliably estimate this parameter.

Estimates of model parameters resulting from fitting a discrete logistic model with MCMC to a time-series of estimated population sizes and harvest rates of mallards breeding in Alaska, 1990–2007.

Parameter	Mean	SD	95% credibility interval
K	1.192	0.306	0.708–1.860
P_0	0.319	0.088	0.205–0.535
d	1.004	0.544	0.070–1.933
r	0.315	0.129	0.099–0.597
σ^2	0.021	0.013	0.005–0.055

California-Oregon mallards

Data selection.—Breeding-population estimates of mallards in California are available starting in 1992, but not until 1994 in Oregon. Also, Oregon did not conduct a survey in 2001. In order to avoid truncating the time-series, we used the admittedly weak relationship ($P = 0.18$) between California and Oregon population estimates to predict population sizes in Oregon in 1992, 1993, and 2001. The fitted linear model was:

$$N_t^{OR} = 80033 + 0.0734\left(N_t^{CA}\right)$$

To derive realistic standard errors, we assumed that the predictions had the same mean coefficient of variation as the years when surveys were conducted ($n = 13$, CV = 0.082). The estimated sizes and variances of the California-Oregon stock were calculated by simply summing the state-specific estimates.

We pooled banding and recovery data for California and Oregon and estimated harvest rates in the same manner as that for Alaska mallards. Although banded sample sizes were sufficient in all years, harvest rates could not be estimated for the years 1996–2001 because of unknown changes in band-reporting rates. As with Alaska, available estimates of harvest rate showed no apparent trend over time, and we simply used the mean and standard deviation of the available estimates and generated independent samples of predictions for the missing years based on a logit transformation and an assumption of normality:

$$\ln\left(\frac{h_t}{1 - h_t}\right) \sim Normal(-1.9844, 0.0351) \quad for \ t = 1996 - 2001$$

Prior distributions for K and P_0.— Unlike the Alaska stock, the California-Oregon population has been relatively stable with a mean of 0.48 million mallards. We believed K should be in the range $0.48 - 0.96$ million, assuming the logistic model and that harvest rates were $\leq r/2$. We therefore specified a prior distribution on K that had a mean of 0.7 million, but with a variance sufficiently large to admit a wide range of possible values:

$$K \sim Log - normal(-0.5628, 0.41224)$$

The estimated size of the California-Oregon stock was 0.48 million at the start of the time-series (i.e., 1992). We used a similar line of reasoning as that for Alaska for specifying a prior distribution P_0, positing that initial population size was 40–100% of K. Thus on a log scale:

$$P_o \sim Uniform(-0.9163, 0.0)$$

Parameter estimates.—The logistic model and associated posterior parameter estimates provided a reasonable fit to the observed time-series of population estimates. The posterior means of K and r were similar to their priors, although the variances were considerably smaller (albeit still large) (Table b). Interestingly, the posterior mean of *d* was <1, suggestive of a compensatory response to harvest; however the standard deviation of the estimate was large, with the upper 95% credibility limit >1.

Estimates of model parameters resulting from fitting a discrete logistic model with MCMC to a time-series of estimated population sizes and harvest rates of mallards breeding in California and Oregon, 1992–2007.

Parameter	Mean	SD	95% credibility interval
K	0.662	0.169	0.452–1.081
P_0	0.732	0.158	0.431–0.983
d	0.616	0.431	0.034–1.649
r	0.357	0.224	0.074–0.919
σ^2	0.014	0.012	0.002–0.045

APPENDIX 5: Modeling Mallard Harvest Rates

We modeled harvest rates of mid-continent mallards within a Bayesian hierarchical framework. We developed a set of models to predict harvest rates under each regulatory alternative as a function of the harvest rates observed under the liberal alternative, using historical information. We modeled the probability of regulation-specific harvest rates (h) based on normal distributions with the following parameterizations:

Closed: $\quad p(h_C) \sim N(\mu_C, v_C^2)$

Restrictive: $\quad p(h_R) \sim N(\gamma_R \mu_L, v_R^2)$

Moderate: $\quad p(h_M) \sim N(\gamma_M \mu_L + \delta_f, v_M^2)$

Liberal: $\quad p(h_L) \sim N(\mu_L + \delta_f, v_L^2)$

For the restrictive and moderate alternatives we introduced the parameter γ to represent the relative difference between the harvest rate observed under the liberal alternative and the moderate or restrictive alternatives. Based on this parameterization, we are making use of the information that has been gained (under the liberal alternative) and are modeling harvest rates for the restrictive and moderate alternatives as a function of the mean harvest rate observed under the liberal alternative. For the harvest-rate distributions assumed under the restrictive and moderate regulatory packages, we specified that γ_R and γ_M are equal to the prior estimates of the predicted mean harvest rates under the restrictive and moderate alternatives divided by the prior estimates of the predicted mean harvest rates observed under the liberal alternative. Thus, these parameters act to scale the mean of the restrictive and moderate distributions in relation to the mean harvest rate observed under the liberal regulatory alternative. We also considered the marginal effect of framework-date extensions under the moderate and liberal alternatives by including the parameter δ_f.

In order to update the probability distributions of harvest rates realized under each regulatory alternative, we first needed to specify a prior probability distribution for each of the model parameters. These distributions represent prior beliefs regarding the relationship between each regulatory alternative and the expected harvest rates. We used a normal distribution to represent the mean and a scaled inverse-chi-square distribution to represent the variance of the normal distribution of the likelihood. For the mean (μ) of each harvest-rate distribution associated with each regulatory alternative, we use the predicted mean harvest rates provided in USFWS (2000:13–14), assuming uniformity of regulatory prescriptions across flyways. We set prior values of each standard deviation (v) equal to 20% of the mean (CV = 0.2) based on an analysis by Johnson et al. (1997). We then specified the following prior distributions and parameter values under each regulatory package:

Closed (in U.S. only):

$$p(\mu_C) \sim N(0.0088, \frac{0.0018^2}{6})$$

$$p(v_C^2) \sim Scaled\ Inv\ \text{-}\ \chi^2(6, 0.0018^2)$$

These closed-season parameter values are based on observed harvest rates in Canada during the 1988–93 seasons, which was a period of restrictive regulations in both Canada and the United States.

For the restrictive and moderate alternatives, we specified that the standard error of the normal distribution of the scaling parameter is based on a coefficient of variation for the mean equal to 0.3. The scale parameter of the inverse-chi-square distribution was set equal to the standard deviation of the harvest rate mean under the restrictive and moderate regulation alternatives (i.e., CV = 0.2).

Restrictive:

$$p(\gamma_R) \sim N(0.51, \frac{0.15^2}{6})$$

$$p(v_R^2) \sim Scaled\ Inv - \chi^2(6, 0.0133^2)$$

Moderate:

$$p(\gamma_M) \sim N(0.85, \frac{0.26^2}{6})$$

$$p(v_M^2) \sim Scaled\ Inv - \chi^2(6, 0.0223^2)$$

Liberal:

$$p(\mu_L) \sim N(0.1305, \frac{0.0261^2}{6})$$

$$p(v_L^2) \sim Scaled\ Inv - \chi^2(6, 0.0261^2)$$

The prior distribution for the marginal effect of the framework-date extension was specified as:

$$p(\delta_f) \sim N(0.02, 0.01^2)$$

The prior distributions were multiplied by the likelihood functions based on the last seven years of data under liberal regulations, and the resulting posterior distributions were evaluated with Markov Chain Monte Carlo simulation. Posterior estimates of model parameters and of annual harvest rates are provided in the following table:

Parameter	Estimate	SD	Parameter	Estimate	SD
μ_C	0.0088	0.0021	h_{1998}	0.1019	0.0070
v_C	0.0019	0.0005	h_{1999}	0.0981	0.0072
γ_R	0.5110	0.0606	h_{2000}	0.1249	0.0085
v_R	0.0129	0.0032	h_{2001}	0.0918	0.0088
γ_M	0.8452	0.1058	h_{2002}	0.1051	0.0043
v_M	0.0216	0.0055	h_{2003}	0.1050	0.0052
μ_L	0.1093	0.0069	h_{2004}	0.1150	0.0077
v_L	0.0207	0.0039	h_{2005}	0.1105	0.0071
δ_f	0.0060	0.0077	h_{2006}	0.1023	0.0066
			h_{2007}	0.0930	0.0055

We modeled harvest rates of eastern mallards using the same parameterizations as those for mid-continent mallards:

Closed: $\quad p(h_C) \sim N(\mu_C, v_C^2)$

Restrictive: $\quad p(h_R) \sim N(\gamma_R \mu_L, v_R^2)$

Moderate: $\quad p(h_M) \sim N(\gamma_M \mu_L + \delta_f, v_M^2)$

Liberal: $\quad p(h_L) \sim N(\mu_L + \delta_f, v_L^2)$

We set prior values of each standard deviation (v) equal to 30% of the mean (CV = 0.3) to account for additional variation due to changes in regulations in the other Flyways and their unpredictable effects on the harvest rates of eastern mallards. We then specified the following prior distribution and parameter values for the liberal regulatory alternative:

Liberal:

$$p(\mu_L) \sim N(0.1771, \frac{0.0531^2}{6})$$

$$p(v_L^2) \sim Scaled\ Inv - \chi^2(6, 0.0531^2)$$

Moderate:

$$p(\gamma_M) \sim N(0.92, \frac{0.28^2}{6})$$

$$p(v_M^2) \sim Scaled\ Inv - \chi^2(6, 0.0488^2)$$

Restrictive:

$$p(\gamma_R) \sim N(0.76, \frac{0.28^2}{6})$$

$$p(v_R^2) \sim Scaled\ Inv - \chi^2(6, 0.0406^2)$$

Closed (in U.S. only):

$$p(\mu_C) \sim N(0.0800, \frac{0.0240^2}{6})$$

$$p(v_C^2) \sim Scaled\ Inv - \chi^2(6, 0.0240^2)$$

A previous analysis suggested that the effect of the framework-date extension on eastern mallards would be of lower magnitude and more variable than on mid-continent mallards (USFWS 2000). Therefore, we specified the following prior distribution for the marginal effect of the framework-date extension for eastern mallards as:

$$p(\delta_f) \sim N(0.01, 0.01^2)$$

The prior distributions were multiplied by the likelihood functions based on the last four years of data under liberal regulations, and the resulting posterior distributions were evaluated with Markov Chain Monte Carlo simulation. Posterior estimates of model parameters and of annual harvest rates are provided in the following table:

Parameter	Estimate	SD	Parameter	Estimate	SD
μ_C	0.0789	0.0257	h_{2002}	0.1621	0.0127
ν_C	0.0233	0.0058	h_{2003}	0.1460	0.0105
γ_R	0.7601	0.1129	h_{2004}	0.1361	0.0114
ν_R	0.0394	0.0100	h_{2005}	0.1310	0.0119
γ_M	0.9210	0.1161	h_{2006}	0.1036	0.0132
ν_M	0.0471	0.0119	h_{2007}	0.1192	0.0134
μ_L	0.1489	0.0157			
ν_L	0.0446	0.0091			
δ_f	0.0039	0.0095			

APPENDIX 6: Scaup Model

We use a state-space formulation of scaup population and harvest dynamics within a Bayesian estimation framework (Meyer and Millar 1999, Millar and Meyer 2000). This analytical framework allows us to represent uncertainty associated with the monitoring programs (observation error) and the ability of our model formulation to predict actual changes in the system (process error).

8.1 Process Model

Given a logistic growth population model that includes harvest (Schaefer 1954), scaup population and harvest dynamics are calculated as a function of the intrinsic rate of increase (r), the carrying capacity (K), along with the harvest (H_t). Following Meyer and Millar (1999), we scaled population sizes by K (i.e., $P_t = N_t/K$) and assumed that process errors (ε_t) are lognormally distributed with a mean of 0 and variance $\sigma^2_{Process}$. The state dynamics can be expressed as

$$P_{1974} = P_0\, e^{\varepsilon_{1974}}$$
$$P_t = \left(P_{t-1} + rP_{t-1}(1 - P_{t-1}) - H_{t-1}/K\right)e^{\varepsilon_t}, t = 1975,...,2007,$$

where P_0 is the initial ratio of population size to carrying capacity. To predict total scaup harvest levels, we modeled scaup harvest rates (h_t) as a function of the pooled direct recovery rate (f_t) observed each year with

$$h_t = f_t / \lambda_t.$$

We specified reporting rate (λ_t) distributions based on estimates for mallards (*Anas platyrhynchos*) from large scale historical and existing reward banding studies (Henny and Burham 1972, Nichols *et. al.* 1995b, P. Garrettson *unpublished data*). We accounted for increases in reporting rate believed to be associated with changes in band type (e.g., from AVISE and new address bands to 1-800 toll free bands) by specifying year specific reporting rates according to

$$\lambda_t \sim Normal(0.38, 0.04) \quad t = 1974,...,1996$$
$$\lambda_t \sim Normal(0.70, 0.04) \quad t = 1997,...,2007.$$

We then predicted total scaup harvest (H_t) with

$$H_t = h_t\left[P_t + rP_t(1 - P)\right]K, t = 1974,...,2007.$$

8.2 Observation Model

We compared our predictions of population and harvest numbers from our process model to the observations collected by the Waterfowl and Breeding Habitat Survey (WBPHS) and the Harvest Survey programs with the following relationships, assuming that the population and harvest observation errors were additive and normally distributed. May breeding population estimates were related to model predictions by

$$N_t^{Observed} - P_t K = \varepsilon_t^{BPOP}, \text{where}$$
$$\varepsilon_t^{BPOP} \sim N(0, \sigma^2_{t,BPOP}), t = 1974,...,2007,$$

where $\sigma^2_{t,BPOP}$ is specified for each year with the variance estimates resulting from the WBPHS.

We adjusted our harvest predictions to the observed harvest data estimates with a scaling parameter (q) according to

$$H_t^{Observed} - \left(h_t\left[P_t + rP_t(1-P)\right]K\right)/q = \varepsilon_t^H, t = 1974,...,2007, \text{ where}$$

$$\varepsilon_t^H \sim N(0, \sigma^2_{t,Harvest}).$$

We assumed that appropriate measures of the harvest observation error $\sigma^2_{t,Harvest}$ could be approximated by assuming a coefficient of variation for each annual harvest estimate equal to 0.15 (Paul Padding *pers. comm.*). The final component of the likelihood included the year specific direct recovery rates that were represented by the rate parameter (f_t) of a Binomial distribution indexed by the total number of birds banded preseason and estimated with.

$$f_t = m_t / M_t,$$
$$m_t \sim Binomial(M_t, f_t)$$

where m_t is the total number of scaup banded preseason in year t and recovered during the hunting season in year t and M_t is the total number of scaup banded preseason in year t.

8.3 Bayesian Analysis

Following Meyer and Millar (1999), we developed a fully conditional joint probability model, by first proposing prior distributions for all model parameters and unobserved system states and secondly by developing a fully conditional likelihood for each sampling distribution.

Prior Distributions

For this analysis, a joint prior distribution is required because the unknown system states P are assumed to be conditionally independent (Meyer and Millar 1999). This leads to the following joint prior distribution for the model parameters and unobserved system states

$$P(r, K, q, f_t, \lambda_t, \sigma^2_{process}, P_0, P_{1, ,T})$$

$$= p(r)p(K)p(q)p(f_t)p(\lambda_t)p(\sigma^2_{Process})p(P_0)p(P_1 \mid P_0, \sigma^2_{Process}) \times \prod_{t=2}^{n} p(P_t \mid P_{t-1}, r, K, f_{t-1}, \lambda_{t-1}, \sigma^2_{Process}).$$

In general, we chose non-informative priors to represent the uncertainty we have in specifying the value of the parameters used in our assessment. However, we were required to use existing information to specify informative priors for the initial ratio of population size to carrying capacity (P_0) as well as the reporting rate values (λ_t) specified above that were used to adjust the direct recovery rates estimates to harvest rates.

We specified that the value of P_0, ranged from the population size at maximum sustained yield ($P_0 = N_{MSY}/K = (K/2)/K = 0.5$) to the carrying capacity ($P_0 = N/K = 1$), using a uniform distribution on the log scale to represent this range of values. We assumed that the exploitation experienced at this population state was somewhere on the right-hand shoulder of a sustained yield curve (i.e., between MSY and K). Given that we have very little evidence to suggest that historical scaup harvest levels were limiting scaup population growth, this seems like a reasonable prior distribution.

We used non-informative prior distributions to represent the variance and scaling terms, while the priors for the population parameters r and K were chosen to be vague but within biological bounds. These distributions were specified according to

$$P_0 \sim Uniform(\ln(0.5),0),$$

$$K \sim Lognormal\ (2.17,\ 0.667),$$

$$r \sim Uniform\ (0.00001,\ 2),$$

$$f_t \sim Beta(0.5,0.5),$$

$$q \sim Uniform(0.0,\ 2),$$

$$\sigma^2_{Process} \sim Inverse\ Gamma\ (0.001,\ 0.001).$$

Likelihood

We related the observed population, total harvest estimates, and observed direct recoveries to the model parameters and unobserved system states with the following likelihood function:

$$P(N_{1,\ ,T}, H_{1,\ ,T}, m_{1,\ ,T}, M_{1,\ ,T} \mid r, K, f_t, \lambda_t, q, \sigma^2_{process}, \sigma^2_{Harvest}, P_{1,\ ,T})$$

$$= \prod_{t=1}^{T} p(N_t \mid P_t, K, \sigma^2_{BPOP}) \times \prod_{t=1}^{T} p(H_t \mid P_t, r, K, f_t, \lambda_t, q, \sigma^2_{Harvest}) \times \prod_{t=1}^{T} p(m_t \mid M_t, f_t).$$

Posterior Evaluation

Using Bayes theorem we then specified a posterior distribution for the fully conditional joint probability distribution of the parameters given the observed information according to

$$P(r, K, q, f_t, \lambda_t, \sigma^2_{process}, P_0, P_{1,\ ,T} \mid N_{1,\ ,T}, H_{1,\ ,T}, m_{1,\ ,T}, M_{1,\ ,T})$$

$$\propto p(r)p(K)p(q)p(f_t)p(\lambda_t)p(\sigma^2_{Process})p(P_0)p(P_1 \mid P_0, \sigma^2_{Process}) \times \prod_{t=2}^{n} p(P_t \mid P_{t-1}, r, K, f_{t-1}, \lambda_{t-1}, \sigma^2_{Process})$$

$$\times \prod_{t=1}^{T} p(N_t \mid P_t, K, \sigma^2_{BPOP}) \times \prod_{t=1}^{T} p(H_t \mid P_t, r, K, q, f_t, \lambda_t, \sigma^2_{Harvest}) \times \prod_{t=1}^{T} p(m_t \mid M_t, f_t,).$$

We used Markov Chain Monte Carlo (MCMC) methods to evaluate the posterior distribution using WinBUGS (Spiegelhalter et al. 2003). We randomly generated initial values and simulated 5 independent chains each with 1,000,000 iterations. We discarded the first half of the simulation and thinned each chain by 250, yielding a sample of 10,000 points. We calculated Gelman-Rubin statistics (Brooks and Gelman 1998) to monitor for lack of convergence. The state space formulation and Bayesian analysis framework provided reasonable fits to the observed breeding population and total harvest estimates with realistic measures of variation. The 2008 posterior estimates of model parameters based on data from 1974–2007 are provided in the following table:

Parameter	Mean	Median	95% Credibility Interval	
r	0.101	0.089	0.023	0.240
K (millions)	8.338	7.982	5.786	12.220
σ^2	0.007	0.006	0.002	0.016
q	0.537	0.536	0.464	0.620